I Talk To Strangers

(to be sure, to be sure, to be sure)

CAROLE CHANDLER

BALBOA.
PRESS
A DIVISION OF HAY HOUSE

*

At last I had organised my trip to Ireland and finally the day had come. I had wanted to visit the Emerald Isles for as long as I could remember. Over and over again I had found myself saying that I wanted to go but had never been and realised that there was nothing stopping me but myself. As the year started I made the decision to stop talking about wanting to go and well, just go.

One of the reasons for my excitement was to see if my joy of talking to strangers was limited to my encounters at home in London. I love meeting people and continue to be surprised and delighted by how people seem to find reasons to chat to me. People come and go and I revel in the pleasure of learning something about myself from every person that I meet. I hear repeatedly that our English capital city is unfriendly, yet strangers speak to me for all manner of excuses. I wondered how experiences might compare in Ireland's capital city. There was only one way to find out.

It was departure day and I woke up with the alarm, which is a rarity for me. I am accustomed to the efficiency of my body clock, now that I have stopped using the unsocial hours of NHS hospital work as my excuse for interrupting my necessary REM sleep. Good grief, no wonder I was ill so often, no wonder I was tired so often, no wonder I was miserable so often. The only issue was that I did not realise it. Sick, tired and miserable were my norm and I had no idea that I could feel different or that life could even be different.

Alarm set for 5.33, eyes opened, bing! Oh joy, I was off to Ireland. It would have been an understatement to say that I was excited. It seemed such a long way ahead when I booked it four months earlier and the day had finally arrived. Yay! I remember booking my trip in January. I sat at my computer and the thought process was clear, where do I want to go, Ireland, what do I want to do, dance, so I searched those two words. Up popped a tango weekend in Dublin in April and after a few minutes browsing their pages, I booked myself on what turned out to be a bit of an adventure. My intention was clear, my primary reason for my holiday was to experience the place and the dancing was a secondary factor.

In the run up I tried to play it cool, tried to play down my excitement and that clearly did not work, for the oddest thing happened the day before departure day, something so very odd that I simply cannot remember the last time it happened. I was late for work. Well I do remember once over twenty years ago, I was late on my first day of a new job, the day after moving home. It was especially annoying as I had done a trial run of the journey the night before, to make sure everything went well, what a pity that plan fell flat on its face. I was late because the clocks changed, thanks to the ever so popular and ever so necessary daylight saving. I was totally unaware, I assume due to my busy schedule in the preceding week.

So, I was late for work the day before my hols. I do not know how and I do not know why. I gave myself two hours for a thirty five minute journey. Admittedly, I made a slight detour to buy a couple of books for my trip but that fails to explain how or why I managed to be twenty minutes late. Anyway, that's enough about all that.

I wanted to be out and on my way by 6.00 but I was not getting out of bed before completing my morning meditation. Why do I meditate every morning? It is my good feeling way to start the day. People tell me that they do not have time to meditate. I suggest that there is value in making time for it. Meditation puts the 'to do' list into perspective and changes priorities. Often seemingly urgent things do not need doing at all.

Just for fun, I had given myself a challenge of doing the same meditation every morning for a month before getting out of bed. This month I set the goal of doing a laughing meditation. Yes, a laughing meditation. I figured that if laughter is the best medicine then I would self-prescribe, self-medicate and treat myself to a jolly start. From the first day I felt myself enjoying the benefits. I started by inhaling deeply, then on the out breath, laughed and laughed, complete with shoulder rolling, stomach grabbing and rib hugging. Well obviously I had to go through the motions, it would have seemed silly without it, right? Seriously though, the more I did it the easier it became. Of course it felt weird at first but it was worth the effort. For thirty three breaths I would just keep going and sometimes my eyes watered and my jaw ached. Funnily enough, it was occasionally hard to stop myself. It proved to be a jolly fun way to start the day. Anyway, with the laughing meditation over, I had other matters to concern me.

I was ready in a flash and left a message for my eighteen year old son in the form of an A5 sheet of paper with a smiley face on it in red felt tip, leaving it in a prominent position i.e. in front of the television, where he would obviously find it. The smiley face encompassed all I wanted to say. There was no need for a 'remember to...' or a 'don't forget to...' I was leaving him alone for the first time and had every confidence that he would be fine and enjoy the break as much as me. Surely, it was only going to do him good to not have me around. It would do him good to wash up occasionally. It would do him good to throw away his empty food packaging. It would do him good to ... you can fill in the blank.

I did not want him to worry. I had been asked the question, "Won't people think it is a bit weird seeing you walking around on your own?" Perhaps it was a fair question but I was not going to worry about that. All I knew was that I was looking forward to my adventure. He was used to me telling him about strangers chatting to me around the town on buses, in the street, in shops, just about anywhere. Would it be the same in Ireland? I had no idea. I shrugged off any concerns. They were unfounded and I have rightly or wrongly never been one to allow such thoughts to cloud my judgement. I was going and that was all there was to it.

Moving on.

*

I walked to the bus stop and the weather was, well, weather. Was it raining? Did anyone care? It kind of dripped around me, not on me but I was used to that, which is just as well because I stopped carrying an umbrella years ago and it has never been an issue. Apart from remembering how much fun it is to use them to accessorise an outfit, I do not miss them at all.

At the bus stop at this early hour with just myself for company, I took advantage of the time and space to resume my laughing. If anyone had seen me I suspect that they may have had an opinion or two about my rocking and grinning. Did I care? Not much. To be fair, I did moderate my behaviour when someone walked past but they were head down all hooded up and at that time of the morning probably would not have noticed me anyway.

Standing at a bus stop served by four routes, three buses arrived at once. I boarded mine, smiled and said hallo to the driver. Yay! He smiled and said hallo back. Now that is always a great start.

Looking out of the window at Clapham Junction I saw a man standing in a shop doorway, he was wearing a long black coat, had a black case and held a long black umbrella. Did my eyes deceive me? Was he wearing a bowler hat? He looked great. As we passed, his bowler hat morphed into a peaked cap. Oh well, never mind, perhaps my imagination was playing games with me again. Interesting to see how his entire look was transformed with a change of my perspective.

On a number 77 to Waterloo I negotiated the stairs with my case with the determination that is necessary on a moving bus, especially as it curved around the first roundabout. I was proud of myself for hanging on, up the stairs, in an effort to limit the possible bruising that may have ensued as I bumped from side to side.

Changing at Waterloo I let the first number 68 go to Euston without me. It did not promise to be much fun as it was already full with many people standing downstairs. Another time yes perhaps I might have ignored the crowds but as this was my holiday I decided to wait.

Arriving at Euston I had already previously told myself that I would like to have breakfast at a branch of one of my favourite restaurant chains. I did not know if there even was one in that location. I considered breaking my journey at Holborn where I had enjoyed eating at one of them on Kingsway but concluded that it would be preferable to eat and rest at the station, mostly because one can never know how long a journey may take at that time of the morning and I had no intention of being at the mercy of our capital's traffic and miss my train. Anyway I passed the Marks and Spencer, looked left and there to my amusement was the name I was looking for. Have I been to Euston station before? Yes. Have I noticed this branch there before? No. I was amused and thankful for the fun of finding what I had asked for.

It transpires that I had stumbled across an Express version. I was not even aware that an Express version existed. The result was a less than familiar experience. I could share reams about the gloomy mood of the server, her unnecessary insistence, her unwelcome persistence, the incorrect delivery of my order, the poor quality of the food and the noisy, squeaky, consistently banging staff door. I was looking forward to my breakfast because I have eaten comfortably and enjoyed their usually delicious menu in various locations all over London, as well as Windsor and Birmingham. However, this visit was so unlike any other which I have ever experienced. I realise that were I to share details it would prove difficult to put a positive spin on it, even for me, so I shall move on.

*

My train for Holyhead was surprisingly quiet. Why surprising? Purely because my attempts to book for the following day had failed as it was fully booked. I was not unduly bothered as it meant that I was forced to leave a day earlier so had an extra day in Ireland. I easily booked another day off work and another day's accommodation and besides, there was obviously an unknown reason for me to leave early. I had fun reminding myself that I had no idea what experiences were in store for me.

My reserved seat was opposite a lady already sat at the table. I was happy to sit with her and she had already smiled and said hallo. However, there was just one other person in the whole carriage, he was right at the other end, so I said,

"No offence but I'll move to another table to give us both more room." She smiled sweetly and seemed unconcerned whether I stayed or not. That was lucky because I had no intention of upsetting anyone. Hey, why would she be upset anyway, I was doing us both a favour.

I was glad that a couple of cheerful female staff walked by at that moment, they helped by explaining the seat reservation signs and pointed out that I could choose to sit just about anywhere.

I found it really easy to relax and one minute into the journey I had already vowed to enjoy more rail travel. A young man sat opposite and plugged in his phone. I was impressed. Impressed because (a) he knew that there were sockets, (b) I did not know there were sockets and (c) sockets are not available on buses. Really, I should enjoy more rail travel, perhaps catch up with the twenty first century. It has been so many years since I have transported myself anywhere by train that I was unaware of changes and improvements. After this trip I feared that my beloved buses and coaches may be over taken, in more ways than one.

Glancing out of the window I spotted a McVities factory and idly mused that it would be a great place to work. Well, I was on holiday so I could dream whatever I liked. On our smooth steady arrival at Milton Keynes, I felt a keen sense of gleeful anticipation, wondering who might board the train, who might sit at my table, who might sit beside me, who might arrive to interact with me. One suited gentleman walked past and the train left.

My visit to the toilet was an adventure all of its own. Every grey panel of wall that I saw looked to me like a toilet door. Trading on memory they were about shoulder width so that was where my expectation lay. There were many buttons, so I pressed some left and right expecting a door to open at some point revealing a cupboard size space with a loo.

I continued to press buttons until one responded. Oh my, what a response it was too. An entire wall, an entire red wall disappeared around a curve revealing a lavatory closet four times the size of any I have ever seen on a train. What was I to think? Perhaps I had accidentally transported myself into another dimension, (well, they do say that anything is possible) or perhaps it was simply one of the aforementioned changes and improvements.

Inside the lavatory craft, I mean closet, I pressed the 'close' button and enjoyed watching the large door curve the other way round me. With signs, notices and instructions everywhere, I pressed the 'lock' button. I was safe. So it seems that time has moved on and I am no longer expected to hold the door closed with my foot while I pee. Whoosh! I heard something spray in the loo before I even used it.

There was no view of the passing track and ballast down below, like back in the old days. Good grief Carole, when was the last time you were on a train? Have there really been so many changes? Or perhaps I was just thinking of my travels of years ago on non-tourist trains in the Indian sub-continent as well as Central and South America. There was no such luxury as modern plumbing. I fondly remembered the skill of squatting over a hole in the train, feeling the air wafting across my exposed nether regions. Yes, time has moved on.

Anyway, back on the Holyhead train, after the event, the 'flush' button treated me to an even louder whoosh, I half expected a fanfare or at least some bell ringing. I loved the soap dispenser, automatic water spray and the urgent hand drier which began before I had washed my hands. I let out a laugh all to myself when I spotted the baby changing tray. I imagined that attempting to clean and change a small wriggly person in this environment may prove to be a most entertaining activity indeed.

Fastening my clothes called for the usual dexterity required on a moving vehicle but also an unusual degree of balance and coordination as I bounced from side to side, holding my trouser zip in one hand and the wall rail with the other. I realised that back in the days when the loos were miniscule it was easier to stand because you could practically reach both sides with your knees at the same time. I am not saying that it was better and this is not a complaint, merely an observation.

Back at my table I settled down to read my Mary Poppins which is a wonderfully good read. It is so full of fun and magic that I wonder why more adults do not treat themselves to this easy form of life enhancing joy. The young gentleman at the table opposite asked me if the train was direct to Holyhead or whether he needed to change. I was able to answer his question because I was going to Holyhead too but he did not know that. When he spoke he gave me a taste of the delicious Irish accent that I was so looking forward to hearing more of, much much more. I remember thinking that he must be a trusting soul because he left his bag at the table when he walked away from his seat and disappeared from the carriage. Perhaps it meant nothing at all, perhaps everyone leaves their bag when they go for wander. I think not.

*

The train stopped for several minutes at Chester, well noticeably longer than at Milton Keynes or Crewe. We set off and the view from the window was much the same as before. Then … they arrived! Phones ringing, voices bellowing, music playing. The matriarch headed the team, she was definitely in charge issuing orders to her assembled entourage, where to sit, who could sit with whom, instructions for bags to be passed around. This was the entertainment that the carriage had been waiting for. She was a strong strident female, clearly not one to mess with. I liked her. Her strong Irish accent intrigued me. I could hear the words she used but the order in which she used them intrigued me even further.

Interestingly, she expertly combined cursing with terms of endearment. I think that is a skill. She spoke and spoke and spoke some more. The others of her clan listened. Occasionally they spoke too but she spoke more, much more. She was clearly the one to be obeyed.

As luck would have it their arrival mayhem settled down and I might have even been able to forget their presence but for the occasional demonstrative yawn, cough or exclamation for no apparent reason. Mind you, I did laugh when she called her son on her mobile phone. Why do I mention it? It is quite usual for a mother to ring her son is it not? Yes. I laughed because he was in the same carriage. At first I tried to make sense of their behaviour, quickly became bored thinking about it at all, then decided to find it hilarious and returned to the pleasure of my Mary Poppins.

Carole Chandler

As we left Rhyll, the instant change of view caught my attention. We passed a couple of fields of static caravans which I assumed were holiday homes, so naturally thought that we were passing a holiday village. Why would anyone choose to holiday like that? Why indeed, in the wind, cold and rain? Then I reminded myself, well why does anyone choose anything? We are all individuals, we are all different, we all like different things for different reasons. Then we passed more and more fields of more and more static caravans. I began to think that these were not holiday homes, they were just homes. Some work had gone into personalising the outside spaces with hedges, fencing, gardens, plants, flowers, rockeries, decorative stones and strategically placed white boulders. One could be forgiven for forgetting that they were caravans except for the tell-tale large red gas cylinders propped up outside them.

Then the view really changed. We had mountains, gorgeous beautiful majestic mountains. Let's hear it for Wales, however, I was more than a little relieved to not be disembarking at Llandudno Junction. I am sure that it is nice enough and well done you, if you live there but as far as I could tell, they were being treated to what looked like a year's worth of rain, all in one hour. Chucking it down? It was ridiculous.

Well I was so busy enjoying the splendour of the mountainous terrain to my left that I would have missed the view of the sea to the right, if I had not heard (well I could not really fail to hear) our glorious matriarchal group leader announce the fact to her subjects. Despite their cacophonous arrival I inwardly thanked her for that.

*

Ooh the sea did look a bit choppy. I trusted that our designated water crossing vehicle would be able to cope. The fields of sheep in the cold wind and rain seemed happy enough. I do love how they never seem to mind the weather. There were so many sheep, sheep everywhere, on the grass, on the flat, on the hills, on the coast. They reminded me of many a comedian and comedy sketch in the spirit of entertainment, that I have heard focus on sheep and the Welsh. It began to make sense. Well not really but there were a lot of sheep.

I was enjoying the view. No, really I was. The railway track was flanked by trees on both sides and even in the rain it was really quite beautiful. To the left, streams, rivers, stone farm buildings, to the right, the choppy sea. Above, we were blessed by the darkest, greyest clouds I have seen since a memorable stormy day visit to Florence in Italy, many moons ago.

The bing bong announcer informed us of our arrival into Bangor, which hoved into view after a long, long, long tunnel. (Ah that reminds me, it really is about time I took the Eurotunnel trip I have been promising myself for ages). A long, long, long tunnel out of the station too, more and more sheep, then out of nowhere a pergola in a beautiful garden with a rockery lined road as its approach. What was that doing there? It looks like a pretty place to visit anyway.

*

With the bing bong announcement for Holyhead, I looked out of the window to see a view dominated by ASDA and McDonald's. Why do I always expect places to look different? In the station it certainly was different. Ouch! I was definitely out of London. I seemed to be causing quite a stir. Furtive glances, more than one or two. I am accustomed to people looking at me, I am accustomed to people staring at me but I am also used to smiling and getting one back in return. That was not happening here. Not sure what was going on but determined to stay in a good feeling emotional place, I endeavoured to view their responses differently.

For my whole life I thought that people looked at me, stared at me and noticed me because there was something wrong with me, or because I was different or because I did not belong. I wasted a lot of time and energy trying to work out what was wrong with me, trying to be same as others or trying to find a way to fit in. I was on a hiding to nothing. I am me but I never allowed myself to be me and never knew what it felt like to be me, so consequently trying to fit in was futile. I mean really, fit in where? Thank goodness I discovered a better way. Thank goodness I found an alternative perspective. Thank goodness I learned the power of following my inner guidance. Of course people look at me, stare at me and notice me. Now I know why.

So there I was at the Pumpkin Café in the passenger terminal and the lovely pleasant lady behind the counter worked really hard serving the queue of waiting travellers with efficiency and courtesy. I chuckled inwardly when she handed me not one but two loyalty cards. How hopeful was that? Sitting on a mini real genuine leatherette sofa which had clearly seen better days, I returned my focus to my hot ham and cheese panini. Well they call it a panini but, firstly, what they called a panini was not a panini, it was a long flat white soft bap roll type offering, secondly, it was heated in a microwave therefore instead of being uniformly hot and toasted with a welcome crunch, it was rubbery, piping hot in the middle and cool on the outside. I am used to paninis crusty and toasted to perfection in a London stylie.

I certainly do not blame the server, she was clearly a gem to the establishment, following heating orders with the equipment provided and deserving an award for working so hard. I may be wrong but I guess it was just a case of offering things the way (they think) the customers want it. Then again who is a customer likely to be? This is a ferry passenger terminal, all types are passing through right? Perhaps I had much to learn.

A family parked beside me, the baby in a buggy chuckled and gurgled excitedly. Was it my imagination or was it gurgling in an Irish accent? The cute baby caught my attention. With mummy in the queue, daddy soothed his daughter by singing his own version of whale inspired sounds. So soothing I nearly dozed off myself, which I fear would not have been difficult given my early start and my thwarted attempts to get some early shut eye the night before, due to my son's desire to play and discuss minutiae. Was he being clingy? Was he missing me already? I do so love how people complain about babies interfering with sleep when teenagers (bless them) do it too.

The sound of a happy baby is always a joy. I glanced across at the father, he responded to my smile with a big cheesy grin spread right across his face. Yay, someone had smiled back. Thank goodness, perhaps I was going to be okay after all, so far from home, so far from my comfort zone.

Mummy arrived armed with snacks. Moving her baby and buggy closer to her I glanced over and in an instant witnessed an expression which is recognisable the world over. It was the unmistakable look of love of a mother for her baby. It was a universal gaze which works in any country, any culture and any language. I enjoyed listening to them speak. The couple's accents were softer and gentler than that of the man pacing back and forth across the café discussing business on his phone, yet I loved it all and looked forward to hearing more.

Deciding to check in I stood up, coat on, scarf and bag at the ready then the announcement began,

"This is an announcement for all Irish Ferries passengers. Irish Ferries regrets to announce that due to the adverse weather conditions ..."

Oh no, not the dreaded 'c' word, no, surely not. Please do not say it. I had gone to all this trouble and come so far and really looking forward to my holiday. I did not want to think about it. Quickly I distracted myself with a 'la la la' in my head, focus Carole, focus, remember that things always work out well for you, remember that all is well.

"... the 14.10 departure will be ..."

'la la la' all is well, all is well

"... delayed by twenty minutes."

Phew, that was close.

*

At the lone check in desk there was a group of kissing, hugging young ladies, so I popped into the loos to give them time to complete their emotional goodbyes. The entrance to the ladies' was past a wall of sky blue and sapphire blue glass tiles. They were bright, dazzlingly bright. Inside the walls were decorated in sky blue and sapphire blue tiles. They were bright, even brighter than the dazzlingly bright outside. The décor was made brighter in the glare of the fluorescent lighting. What was all that about? I never knew that toilet paper could look blindingly white and this blue white light was fierce on the eyes. I could not wait to get out. Perhaps that was the idea.

Back at the check in desk, retinas intact, the kissing and hugging youngsters were still in action. I waited patiently until they broke apart eventually amidst a sea of 'thank you for ...' and 'let us know when ...' and 'promise to ...' etc etc. The bright lady at the desk politely and efficiently dealt with my check in procedure. Now then, having worked for several years in the busy international terminal 3 of our wonderful Heathrow airport, I found this ferry passenger terminal rather quaint.

I gave her my ferry ticket but she also requested my railway ticket. No doubt she had her reason, I just do not know why she needed it and I did not bother to ask. She asked if I had bags to check in and I was surprised. For some reason I did not think that happened on a ferry, I simply thought that passengers kept their luggage with them. Oh so much to learn and so little time. I say that a little tongue in cheek as I understand that time is an illusion so there is always enough time for anything and everything.

She looked at my case and made the decision for me, saying that I could keep it with me. Little did I know that there would be stairs and escalators and multiple walkways to negotiate and life would be considerably easier without a case but never mind I valued her wisdom and was ready to proceed. Even if I say it myself, my black, patent leather, mock croc case is rather beautiful so is a joy to wheel around, like an accessory coordinated with my shoes and bag.

After she printed my boarding pass, with my name on it, I wandered off not sure which way to go, as there did not seem to be much in the way of signs to direct me. Also, there were no passengers to follow so I just kept going until someone shouted "this way". Two lovely smiling reflective jacket clad gentleman waved me through. Turning a corner I met a bunch of people at the end of the concourse. As I approached, it appeared that no one was moving. What were they waiting for? There were four rows of seats but they were all standing and waiting. I could not see the point so I sat down. I thought, well, if I am going to wait, I may as well sit. I looked around and when I turned back they had all disappeared, all that is except one man and member of staff.

I moved forward expecting to see the walkway for the ship, only to discover that the waiting people were now on a bus. I said to the uniformed chappy,

"Oh, I'm just looking around, wondering how this all works. Are we going by bus to the ship?"

The other man was a passenger who instead of keeping his recently issued boarding pass handy for inspection, had somehow buried it deep in his bag. Presumably it had not intentionally been buried but had rendered itself difficult to find, due to his unsuccessful rummaging.

He seemed happy enough and while searching told me that I would be fine, they would let me board but he was probably not going to be allowed out of the building. He had quite a sense of humour with his lovely Irish accent, given that his boarding pass was still choosing not to reveal itself. The uniformed chap seemed more relieved than the passenger, when a screwed up version of a boarding card emerged. How did it get into such a state? We were both given a quick explanation about why the tickets must be carefully scrutinised, especially the date. Seemingly, people had found old expired, discarded ones on the floor or on seats and had attempted to use them to travel. Well who would have thought it?

We sat beside each other on the last two seats of the bus and he of the screwed up ticket amused us all with further displays of his great sense of humour and ready wit. He endeavoured to hold a conversation with a little girl travelling with her mother. Most of what he said was misunderstood by both the girl and her mother, who offered frequent displays of her short fuse and a liberal sprinkling of intolerance, as she laughed at her daughter but not with her. Conversely, our lovely Irish gent showed admirable patience as the girl asked frequent repeated questions. I found it interesting to witness how the girl responded calmly to him but not to her parent.

Arriving at the ferry I still expected to walk from a path up a plank type walkway to the deck but no, our bus drove on board. I was the last one off the bus along with the ticket rummager. We followed the group of foot passenger to the stairs where this lovely, lovely, charming gentleman promptly turned and picked up my case announcing that he would carry it for me. He then said,

"It might kill me but I'm determined to carry it anyway". Oh how funny is that? When I told this sequence of events to friends on my return, someone suggested that he might have run off with my case, now really, why would he have done that?

He raced up the stairs at a pace calling back at me, "Keep up, there are more flights to go". Well this ship was certainly bigger than I was expecting. At the top, after all of those stairs, turning, walking, turning and walking, this lovely charming gentleman made some quip about surviving, although he seemed wonderfully strong to me. I thanked him for his kindness, he was a real gentleman. I considered bringing the word chivalry into my spoken gratitude but decided that may be a step too far. I thanked him, he walked away and disappeared somewhere on the ship and I never saw him again. He had carried my case, no ulterior motive just kindness. People really are quite lovely aren't they?

*

The sign for the on board cinema induced excitement within me. I love the cinema, I had no idea what they were showing but I wanted some of that. People were milling about gathering in clumps, oddly sitting in the same area, when there were other areas with more space and much quieter. I love how people do that, sit with others in a public space then complain about crowds.

The cinema was not open yet, with no staff around but the posters said 'The Muppet Movie' and 'Streetdance 2'. I did not mind or care which one and had decided to enjoy passing a large proportion of my sea crossing time being entertained by moving pictures. A chap sat by himself beside the entrance. With no one else around I asked him if he was waiting to for the film.

"Oh no, I'm just sitting here because it's quiet. I'm just happy reading my book". Well, not only did he look happy enough, he looked nice enough and honest enough so I left my case with him while I toured the deck to find someone who might know how or when I might enjoy my sea movie experience.

The well-dressed attentive staff in the shop directed me to the information desk. The well-dressed attentive staff at the information desk directed me to the shop. I spotted a tall bulky man in ship attire and asked him about the promised movie magic, though I do not suspect I used those actual words. Satisfied with his knowledge and response I returned to my bag in the care of the happy enough, nice enough, honest enough looking guy, to await the opening of the ticket office. My suitcase minder seemed pleased to see me and with a twinkle in his eye said,

"So you'll get to see The Muppet Movie after all." I knew he was joking and felt the urge to tell him that I would happily see either. Given the choice, my preference was for the dance movie but I was content either way because I love animation, I love kids' movies so the Muppets would have been fine too.

Another chap floated by and sat near us. I had vaguely spotted him earlier near the shop. Always open to possibilities and ever wondering what the Universe has in store for me, it was nice to see him turn up so soon. He asked about the film and upon discovering that there was a charge, he up and left. Well, that was interesting. Here was such a cute, handsome, fit looking man so interesting in many ways except in his lack of awareness of his natural abundance. I reminded myself that a man who is concerned about spending a few squids on seeing a movie to pass the time was not my target market, so I did myself a favour and forgot all about him. The waiting time gave me the opportunity for note taking, people watching and focus.

In the meantime, finding the loo was a pleasant surprise. Why surprise? Well, surprise because they were cleaner than any I have seen anywhere on a moving vehicle or anywhere even remotely linked with moving vehicles i.e. stations, airports, terminals. Yes, I was pleasantly surprised. I did wonder if the hand drier suppliers have a sense of humour though, the machines were called 'Tempest' and I am not sure that is really the name that one wants for equipment on a ship.

*

With time to eat before my much anticipated cinematic extravaganza, I queued for hot food at a café to discover from the well-dressed attentive staff that the choice of hot food consisted of pizza or pizza. As my body is a temple, I searched for and found another eating area flanked by arcade machines. Okay, I was not actually searching for the arcade machines, they were there anyway, no doubt a welcome bonus for some.

It was easy to make my choice of rice and vegetables because I had no wish to subject myself or more specifically, my alimentary tract to an unfamiliar intake of chips, burgers, battered fish or fare of that ilk. Frankly my constitution would have no idea what to do with it and being away from home I calculated that it was probably not a risk worth taking. Having said all that, I was really making the best of the availability as my vegetables were of the frozen peas, beans, corn, soggy broccoli and squishy diced carrot variety, so probably or positively not to my usual standard. Ah well, never mind, when in Rome … (to a degree).

Back at the cinema, the film was due to start and there was still no sign of a ticket seller, no sign of anything much happening really. Where was everyone? Another guy arrived, not waiting for the film but also happy to find somewhere to read his book away from the other areas of manic mayhem. I saw his point having walked past people sprawled across benches, children running, parents shouting and couples squabbling. My decision to while away some time watching a dance movie now seemed like money well spent. Still it begged the question, where was everyone?

Yay! The ticket sales cupboard magically opened from the inside. The seller was thin, very thin, with his clothes hanging off him. As Mary Poppins says about someone she met *'he was a long thin man, so thin that he seemed to have no front to him but only two sides'*. Anyway, here was I in geographical limbo and it was fun to be asked which currency I would like to use for payment. Handing over my first Euro note I examined the change much to his amusement. I told him that this money was new to me and he responded with,

"It's all only money, it's all the same just counting from one to a hundred". I agreed but it still looked new and different.

Settling down to watch a spot of dancing I had the whole cinema to myself. I had no one to share the experience with but equally no one to spoil my experience either. I was not expecting much, a fairly tolerable cheesy flick with some fair to middling dance scenes and a loose, vague plot would have sufficed. However, it was heaps better than that, no really it was another pleasant surprise and I quite enjoyed it. I was in my element at my private viewing with my bag, case, coat and shoes all spread out, not to mention stretching myself out across the seats. I happily laughed out loud without fear of complaint and found it a most entertaining way to spend my ferry time.

The cinema experience was complete, my joy was had and my stomach required attention again. Seemingly, the earlier rice and veg combo had not done much in the way of providing sustenance. Not inclined to wander too far I returned to the café, saw the sandwiches which looked nice then noticed a sign for paninis. Always preferring hot food to cold, regardless of the weather I waited until the lone server had finished attending to the customer ahead of me.

The staff member was a tall, slender, beautiful, fine featured girl with hair neatly tied back. Her dark eyes looked at me, we had made eye contact, I smiled, I smiled a big smile. I was feeling great (well the movie had proved to be most entertaining). I smiled and paused. Nothing. No response. No response at all. She looked at me almost as though I was not there. Never mind. I thought nothing of it. Gone are the days when I reacted to the lack of response to my well-meaning smile. Gone are the days when I would think that there was something wrong with me when it happened. Gone are the days when I would think that there was something wrong with her. Now I know better, now I know that I am as I am, she is as she is, we are as we are and that is all great.

Asking for the choice of panini fillings available she said, "cheese and ham" in a voice so distant and unconnected that it reminded me of disembodied voices used for phone recordings of days gone by. Even today, pre-recorded phone voices are friendly and personable, not so this young lady standing before me. I continued to look at her and smile. On reflection, perhaps I should have asked her to clarify whether she was offering cheese and ham or cheese 'n' ham in the style of the inimitable Victoria Wood as her Bren dinner lady character. I wonder if my ferry panini lady would have appreciated the humour? Oh well, I did not think of it at the time so it is too late now anyway.

Not wishing to repeat the day's earlier episode of hot ham and cheese in a soft white inadequately heated cheese bap, masquerading unsuccessfully as a panini, I settled for the turkey bloomer, cold but it would have to do. I chose a vacant table to enjoy my sandwich and a cup of hot water as this appeared to be the second eating zone on board which I discovered did not offer herbal tea. Strange indeed.

*

The boat began to jolt, it was making unpleasant noises. I did not feel comfortable with this new unsteadiness. It was different to the inclement weather inspired rocking we had been subjected to throughout the journey so far. The jolting continued. I did not like it. Was the boat in trouble? Were we in trouble? I chose not to entertain the idea and reminded myself that all was well. I know it is.

Then just about everyone in the café stood up, it was weird to see them move en masse. Again I tried not to be concerned but they seemed to be mobilising. Were they worried too? What did they know? The ship announcement revealed all. We had arrived. Ah, so that was what all the jolting was about. Phew, I wished I had known.

Passengers with cars all congregated in one area and I followed the instructions for foot passengers to wait by the stairs. There hardly seemed any point standing with a crowd of people when there were so many seats available close by, so I parked myself on a bench where it was considerably quieter, still within sight of the herds waiting to descend. When I heard a voice say,

"Hallo there", I turned to see the lovely gorgeous young man from the train, he added, "I was beginning to think you were following me". Okay, before I continue, let me just point out how utterly ridiculous it seems for anyone to suggest that I might have followed them, so ridiculous on many levels. That may have been true if we were talking about the old me. I speak not of the times I have been distracted by a whiff of a particular aftershave detected on a passing man in the street, I have definitely been known to follow a chap or two in those circumstances but that was eons ago, I was young, I was reckless. It may have been possible if we were talking about the previous, insecure me, the unaware me, the undervalued me, the misunderstood me. I refer to times before I discovered how to be me and allow my light to shine.

Anyway, that Carole has gone and been replaced by the Carole who I love so much now and know so well now. She is able to let comments and suggestions pass by, even ridiculous comments and suggestions. It was actually a harmless remark and just used as an excuse to talk to me. The mere fact that it stirred up so much within me is just a reminder that there is always work, personal work to be done. Focus Carole, focus. Remember who you are, remember that everyone means well, remember that people really like you and you have fun wherever you go.

In response, I gently pointed out that I had not seen him the whole time we were on the ship, so it was unlikely that I was following him.

He said, "You walked past me a couple of times and I thought that you looked pretty chilled out". Oh really, is that what he thought? I was surprised and wondered what made him think that, although I did not feel inspired to ask. He continued,

"Yes and I thought the same about you on the train". Well, that was even more of a surprise because I was convinced that he had not even noticed me on the train and there he was forming wonderful opinions of me. I was still at a loss to understand why he found me 'pretty chilled out' when I was not doing anything but reading my book. Someone told me that he probably formed that opinion simply because I was just quietly reading my book but I pointed out that there is little else to do on a train. Anyway, it turns out that I was wrong, as demonstrated by fellow passengers on my return journey. I shall come to them later, much later.

*

So here was this delightful young man, not to mention handsome and slim, okay I have mentioned it, he was handsome and slim, also not to mention friendly and charming, okay I have mentioned it, he was friendly and charming. His winning smile did not go unnoticed and mmm... his Irish accent went a long way towards reducing me to a state of auditory bliss. If such a condition does not exist then perhaps it should.

How nice to meet someone so easy and comfortable to talk to. How nice to meet someone and enjoy flowing conversation. We talked and talked. He showed interest in what I had to say, complimenting me readily. I was interested in what he had to say and threw a few compliments in his direction too.

He lived in Dublin and was returning after a few days of staying with friends in London. However, it turns out that on his first visit to our capital, he had intended to be there for the weekend and loved it so much that he stayed for two years. I have no idea how that even works but he sounded like a fun person with a sense of adventure. Given his demonstration of impulsiveness and spontaneity I wonder why he was so impressed that I was travelling to Ireland on my own but impressed he certainly was. I could have told him that I was on my own but not alone. I could have told him that I was on my own but not lonely. I could have told him that I may have appeared to be alone but I had all the company I needed. I concluded that the moment was neither the time nor place for that conversation.

Carole Chandler

I had fun telling him that I have wanted to visit Ireland for—ever and made the decision at the beginning of the year to stop talking about it and 'just do it'. He liked that. I told him that I had learned a long time ago that if I wait for other people before I do anything or go anywhere then it may never happen. He congratulated me on my attitude to life and for making the decision to 'just do it'. I had already congratulated myself so it was really nice to hear it from someone else and a stranger at that. How wonderful.

I became quite excited while talking to him, not just because he was paying attention to me and not just because he was easy on the eye but because it was dawning on me that I was actually in Ireland, I had actually arrived. Yay! Telling myself to breathe, breathe, breathe and calm down I apologised to him for my excitedness.

He laughed and said, "No no, it's okay, it's okay to be excited, you're on holiday." What a sweetie.

We talked about the possible, probable and positive plans for my stay, the district I was booked to stay in, the tango festival I was taking part in, the sight-seeing tours I had on my list. He kindly gave me advice on buses, trains and general information about getting around. He asked if I had plans to visit areas other than Dublin and mentioned Galway in particular. Well many people have suggested Galway but I told him the same as I told them, that my intention was to visit County Wicklow more than anywhere else, having heard a lot about it I wanted to visit and experience that area.

Why Co. Wicklow? Well, many years ago I attended a residential meditation course way out in the wilds of Somerset, where I met a group of lovely Irish ladies who adopted me as their honorary Irish sister. I spent most of my free time hanging around with them and enjoying their delicious accents and they were the ones who suggested Wicklow as the place for me. Bowing to their superior knowledge I had not considered anywhere else, regardless of how many times people suggested Galway first.

Anyway, I digress. So there we were a chit chat chatting, almost forgetting why we were there, when a crew member asked us to leave because everyone else had gone. We were so busy deep in conversation that we had not even noticed. At the top of the stairs he offered to carry my case and took it at the same time, which was lucky because I was more than happy to accept his kind and thoughtful offer. He introduced himself with a strong and hearty handshake and while enjoying his twinkly eyes, I remember thinking that I was already enjoying my introduction to the Emerald Isles.

Our excited easy flowing conversation continued as we walked down the stairs. I was especially grateful that he felt inspired to continue to assist me, by carrying my suitcase down the two sets of non-moving escalators because I had enough trouble getting myself down. The tread lines play havoc with my eyes, do crazy things with my perspective and mess with my head, so not carrying my bag myself was a huge help.

I waited at immigration expecting to show my passport but the lovely man behind the desk simply asked my nationality, seemed happy with my response and waved me through without seeing my passport. Interesting.

Turning the corner there was my new buddy, bless him for waiting for me, I had not expected him to wait and it was so nice that he did. We walked around another corner together and there at the door was his friend. They greeted each other warmly with big smiles and cheerful voices that I imagined theirs to be a strong friendship based on years of togetherness and shared experiences. Friendships like that do not come easily.

Within moments I was meeting the friend and blow me if he was not just as handsome, just as slim, just as friendly, just as charming with an equally winning smile and with an equally auditorially intoxicating Irish accent. With a hand shake as strong and as hearty as his pal's, I felt blessed and honoured to have met them both.

Carole Chandler

I was immediately introduced, "This is Carole I met her on the boat, this is her first visit to Ireland". After being told where I was heading, the friend said without a moment's hesitation that he knew where it was, had brought his car and would give me a lift. Well with a cough and a splutter it was hard to contain my surprise. The proverbial feather could have easily knocked me down. Were they the nicest people in the world? I was grateful and really appreciated their kindness, not least because the cold, wind and rain showed little sign of abating.

Once again my case was taken for me. They made it clear that they were happy to help because they wanted me to have a nice introduction to my first day in their country. Well what could I say? They were both excellent advertisements for these friendly people. The drive doubled as a bit of a guided tour, some of which I remembered, some of which I did not, all of which was fun. Together they gave me information about the different districts, gave me locations for parks, gardens, galleries and theatres, taught me some slang words, as well as an Irish welcome phrase and I was given further help and advice for easy travel around the city.

They shared an understanding, a knowing, a wonderful sense of mutual interest and appeared so lovely and caring together that I wondered if they had known each other since childhood, school perhaps but no, they only known each other for two and a half months. I was really surprised. I have known brothers with far less of a connection. I was then and still am impressed by their bond. How wonderful to enjoy a friendship like that.

"the bond that links your true family is not one of blood but of respect and joy in each other's life. Rarely do members of one family grow up under the same roof" Illusions – Richard Bach

We arrived, they returned my bag, we parted amidst hugs and thanks and best wishes. Wow, what an introduction, what a wonderful start to my holiday, I felt great, I felt really great.

*

My arrival procedure was easy at reception, the check in was complete, the room sorted and would have been perfect if the radiator had not gone on strike. Well there was no way I was going to survive a week in this fabulous old character building, with its fabulous old character windows, singing along with the wind and rain for accompaniment.

Back at reception, the lovely Irishman who had dealt so efficiently with my arrival had been replaced by a lovely Lithuanian. His accent was fun too but not doing it for me. My room was changed swiftly from a teeny single, to a twin with massive wardrobes and about four times the floor space. Wow, this will do nicely I thought.

My stomach required attention. Not deterred by the rain I walked along the beautiful double tree lined avenue with its fine houses in search of a Chinese take away. I did not know where I was going and just felt inclined to see where my instincts took me. A quarter of an hour later I found one on a main road. My intention to take food back was changed when I saw that the Chinese/Thai restaurant was empty and it looked lovely. It was not at all shabby for Carole.

I enjoyed a set meal of three courses of delicious food and was in no hurry to eat my soup, followed by some form of chicken and rice. It made sense to pause before continuing with my tasty mint and chocolate ice cream, so I took my own sweet time and was in there for a couple of hours reading and writing, while couples and families came, ordered, ate and left. Time and space to write gave me the opportunity to bash out several pages of tools and techniques all for the purpose of feeling good. I was really comfortable, no one bothered me. I surprised myself.

The whole eating out alone experience is relatively new for me and I have a select few places at home where I know I will be happy to go alone and eat alone. Here was I in another country with transferable skills. Just another example of how life is so much easier when you are in a good feeling emotional place.

Walking back in the rain was no big deal. I was in Ireland and happy to be in Ireland and did not care at all. It would have been an understatement to say that I slept well after such a day.

*

What a wonderful start to my next day. I slept like a dream, woke up feeling fantastic wondering what wonderful surprises and experiences the Universe had in store for me. My intention for my first day in this wonderful country was to visit Co. Wicklow. Nothing, absolutely nothing was going to distract me. Wicklow was my goal, Wicklow was my focus.

Already armed with a three day rambler card which I had bought on the way back from the restaurant the previous evening, I found my way to the bus stop in no time and waited near the group of people already there. Then I sensed some minor discomfort as someone approached and then another. Oh dear, I seemed to be causing some confusion as I had not actually joined the neat and tidy line of people to continue the neat and tidy queue. It seemed that the people arriving after me were unclear of where I was supposed to be and that was what I felt. They actually left a space for me and when I realised what was going on I took my place. People smiled and all was well.

So what was my excuse? I am a civilised member of a civilised society, I know how to queue. Well yes I do but let us not forget that I am from London. We do not actually queue for buses in London. We operate by the unwritten rule where people kind of hang around in the general vicinity of the bus stop area, obviously without standing too close to anyone else, sometimes facing different directions. It is the generally accepted social convention to kind of wander about back and forth, with no specific aim, while waiting for a bus arrival. I speak of regular activity frequently witnessed at any stop in our capital city, particularly as we are used to stops serving several routes. No one has any idea which bus other people are waiting for, so it is common to see people waiting in a disassembled, scattered huddle.

When the bus arrives people board in no particular order, certainly very few people care or pay any attention to whether one person was at the stop before another. I am often intrigued by the obvious pecking order of age and gender for some, which can be interesting and highly amusing on occasions. It happens sometimes when a group of unconnected women offer each other the opportunity to board first with the unspoken implication of seniority (i.e. age) first. I love it when I am invited to board before a smiling gesturing gentleman of any age and I am always happy to be acknowledged and accept the act of chivalry, if indeed chivalry is intended.

So where was I? Ah yes, embarking on my first highly anticipated local bus adventure with local people in Dublin and I had learned a lesson already. People queue in an orderly fashion there. It was busy, it was 7.55 am, it was rush hour. I had not even considered that it might be rush hour. I mean for goodness sake, what was I thinking? If I were to wait for public transport anywhere at home at around eight in the morning, on any weekday, I would naturally expect the roads to be busy and people to be waiting. Here was I in a European capital city, of course people had to go to work. I was on holiday but they were not. Life goes on right? Again, what was I thinking? Why did I forget this simple fact? To be fair I had only arrived a few hours previously and had some (albeit minor) adjustments to make.

There was a line of about twenty cars at the traffic lights, with more continually arriving. This the same road which I had walked along the night before for over half an hour to and from my Thai extravaganza, this was the same road where I hardly saw a vehicle the whole time.

*

Call me strange if you like but when I saw the bus coming I felt a sudden burst of excitement. I cannot explain it so I am not going to try but I know I love buses. I find excuses to travel by bus at home and love visiting new cities and travelling on their buses trying out their systems and networks, their little differences, their individual oddities.

Hey do not get me wrong, I have no interest in collecting books with vehicle numbers, I have no interest in joining clubs to discuss route changes, vehicle manufacturing, production, specification or decline. I have no interest in applying for special dispensation to visit bus garages. How could I? I do not even own an anorak. Oh dear, I suspect I may have blown my cover. How do I know so much about obsessive vehicle spotting? Perhaps that is a story for another day. I said perhaps.

Anyway, the bus hoved into view, it was not a majestic red double decker but one of three colours. It looked equally majestic in sky blue, sapphire blue and yellow. What a great colour scheme, I was loving it already. Watching it approach between the double rows of beautiful trees on both sides of the wide avenue where we waited, made the bus look quite grand indeed.

It arrived. It stopped. People got off, passing people getting on via the one door. People paying the driver moved to the left while people using travel cards, bleeped them on the sensor on the right. I watched, I copied, it was strange. It felt strange and I was amused. The pre bus arrival queuing procedure seemed all very orderly and specific. However, the on off procedure seemed less orderly and specific.

I was told a couple of days later that the single door option deterred fare dodgers. That may be so but I have never seen anyone try to board via the exit door on a bus in London. Of course I am not including the triple door bendy bus fiasco, we all know hardly anyone paid on those. They were a gift to fare dodgers and it was hilarious to see people get on at the back and wave their hand in front of the oyster card reader while making the bleeping sound with their voice. The first time I saw someone do that I thought it was an ingenious idea, probably because I had not thought of it myself.

Anyway, I suppose my reaction to the single door was my initial impression. I travelled on so many buses during my stay that I soon became used to it and found that it actually worked efficiently enough so why not just have one door, why not have people flowing past each other on and off? Yeah, why not?

I sat downstairs after asking the driver to let me know the best stop for Grafton Street and we set off taking the first turning off the main road to take some circuitous route to the city. I had only been in Dublin less than a day and already knew that we were not taking a direct set of roads to the centre. It was much like being on my local bus which thankfully has a stop in the middle of my newly built luxury development and is particularly welcome when carrying shopping or after a night out dancing. However, it does take a long route from start to finish and includes not one but two hospitals. When I say includes, it drives around the grounds, much to the annoyance of passengers on a regular basis. I do not bother to complain about it, I am just grateful that it runs at all.

So there I was on my hols on a bus round residential streets, houses and parks more houses and more parks, no shops for ages. Somewhere en route the driver was replaced by another. Why do I bother mention this? Simply

44

because I had asked the first driver to let me know where to get off for the hotel which was my collection point for my tour. He agreed and I was feeling hopeful. So much for my plan then, as he disappeared, so my promise of a heads up disappeared right along with him.

I was loving being on a local bus with local people, real people having real conversations. Well I was in another country and interested to hear what people talk about. A couple of ladies chatted behind me and a chap talked on the phone in front of me. They had a lot to say about roadworks, traffic, weather, friends, neighbours and work. Well, there was a surprise, topics much the same as home really.

Using my intuition I decided when to ask the driver for the best place to get off and guess what? It was the next stop. It was great to know that my inner guidance works at home and away.

*

I was feeling less confident that I would make it to the hotel collection point in time because it had taken me much longer to get to the city than I had anticipated. So it seemed a sensible idea to pop into a tourist information office which was right beside me. I was glad that I did because the young lady confirmed that, while the hotel was indeed one of the places where the coach picks passengers up for the tour, advance booking was essential in case the tour was full. She rang them, I waited, they confirmed, I paid my deposit, I thanked her and left following her directions to the tour bus stop around the corner from the office.

As I had no idea how long I might be on a coach, I popped into a pretty pub, smiled sweetly at the lovely chap who kindly directed me to their toilet. It was all very clean and once again I was nearly blinded by the harsh fluorescent lighting with its powerful blue white light and more glowing toilet paper. Really, seriously, what is that all about? I guess it stops people hanging around, I know I would not want to. I thanked them again and left, found the tour bus stop with lots of posters about the variety of in town and out of town tours available, including a couple for Wicklow. I was hopeful, I was confident, I was happy. I waited and waited and waited.

I do not wear a watch, I stopped wearing a watch a few years ago, roughly when I discovered that time is an illusion, I let go of the need to know the chronological designation of every moment of every day. Apart from missing out on the beauty of watches as jewellery I do not miss them at all. If I feel the urge to know the exact hour of the day, there is always a time telling device of some description available not too far away.

I was standing by a row of shops and the clock outside one of them told me that the coach was scheduled to have arrived already. It may have been late and I had no issue with that, I mean why would I? I was on my hols and nothing much mattered. It was merely a case of deciding how long to wait. How punctual are they in Ireland? What if I returned to the office and it came, then I would miss it. What if? What if? I did not really want to get swept away by what ifs, as experience has proven that a 'what if' frame of mind rarely achieves anything beneficial.

A city tour bus pulled up beside me and I asked the driver for help. Oh what an absolute treasure he was. Like a man waiting for a mission he sprang into action, telling me that I had missed the bus where I was standing but that it was still collecting people and he had seen it around the corner and if I just went back down this road and took a left past the Molly Malone statue then took a right I could not miss it and it was a pink coach and it had Wicklow Tours written on the side of it and it was there and he knew because he had just passed it and he would call them for me to tell the driver that I was on my way and it was not far and he was sure that I would make it and he hoped I would have a lovely day and even though it was raining a little it was a lovely part of the country that I was going to and he was ringing them immediately for me to make sure the driver knew I was coming to ask the driver to wait for me and … and ... and ... and ...

Phew, he talked a lot, he talked fast and he really wanted to help. Like I said he was an absolute treasure.

I hurried down the road and took a left past the statue but all I could see was a confusing network of roads and nothing resembling a pink coach. When I say hurried, it was hurrying for me, I do not run, I certainly do not run for transport, I stopped doing that many years ago. I stopped about the time I stopped wearing a watch, about the time I discovered that time is an illusion anyway. Yes, I am aware that I have already said that but it is worth saying again and I have every confidence that I may feel inclined to repeat it. Changing my view of time has been instrumental in transforming my view of life and has a great deal to do with my self-improvement.

Somehow I found myself back at the tourist office, where I gave the lass a brief account of recent events and she was less than pleased. Apparently, the driver was directing me to the wrong bus as the one he had seen was for a different tour company. Apparently, I had been waiting at the wrong stop. Apparently, I had not followed her directions correctly. Apparently, she had told me where to wait with clear instructions. Apparently, she had told me to wait outside the church. Apparently, I had waited outside the right church but by the wrong stop. Apparently, I had misunderstood. Apparently, it should have been obvious to me that I was waiting in the wrong place. Apparently, the Wicklow Tours posters where I had waited were nothing to do with the tour she had booked for me. Apparently, I should have been aware of that. Apparently, the bus had gone without me. Apparently I had missed it.

Okay okay, I am not saying she was cross. I am not saying she scolded. I am not saying she was seriously displeased. I am not saying that she spoke with unveiled condescension. What I am saying is that I do not speak to my children like that and it is a good many years since I have been on the receiving end of such a tone.

So what did I do? I reminded myself why I was there. I reminded myself that she is not essential to my experience. I reminded myself not to allow the action of another to be my excuse to not feel good. I reminded myself of my goals, 1) to be in joy and 2) to visit Wicklow. I made the decision to regain my composure. I took one long, slow, deep inhalation, paused, then one long, slow, slow, slow exhalation. That was sufficient and I was able to focus again.

Another tour was found, the phone call was made, the place was booked, directions were given, (detailed and clear for a visiting tourist new to the city) and with a "hurry along now" I left. I would not have minded if ... oh never mind Carole, in the words of the great Paul McCartney, *'Let it be'.*

*

Yay! Back around the corner, I found my red mini bus with a lovely, cheerful driver with his clipboard in the rain. He seemed very pleased to see me. Hey, I was pleased to see him too, in case I have not mentioned it, I was really looking forward to going to Wicklow. No need to hurry, seemingly we had plenty of time and he was more than happy to help me on board. He was such a darling and hoped I did not mind my seat being at the back of the bus. All the others were taken and there was just one more passenger to collect after me. Did I mind? Not one bit. After all I had been through already that morning, still only 9.45am I was glad to be finally in with a real chance of actually making to the much anticipated Wicklow. Oh yes.

The driver assisted me up the back step of the bus, how sweet, he announced to the waiting people that I was the last but one passenger, a few people turned around and smiled and one lady said "welcome". Well how nice is that? I am used to people being nice to me and even saying hallo once in a while but I was quite overcome by the spoken welcome and felt a little emotional.

We set off to collect the final passenger. Our bus stopped outside a hotel. A chap climbed on board through the back door just like me. The remaining seat was next to me so he had no choice.

I heard a friendly, "Hi there, you doing okay?" I looked up to be greeted by a vision of beauty, sheer beauty. A tall, young, handsome, blond man was before me. I think I did very well to contain myself. I tried not to think about the very small fact that this divine creature was going to have the pleasure of my company for the next few hours and I was already grateful to the Universe for sending me such a gift.

Our driver, our friendly, informative driver, was clearly happy and proud of his work. No amount of training could teach anyone to deliver the way our driver did. He was a natural and certainly gave the impression that there was no other place or time he would rather be than right there, right then on that bus with all of us. What a blessing to have found myself in the company of such a joyful personality.

The driver's delicious Irish accent was working wonders for me and really getting me in the mood for enjoying my long day out. I chuckled to myself when I noticed that the music playing on the radio station was *'life is what you make it'* along with *'don't worry 'bout a thing, just sing'*. How appropriate.

We were treated to snippets of information and nuggets of humour about a few of the sights we saw on the way out of the city and before long we were surrounded by trees, with a glorious view of hills, streams, waterfalls, lakes, peat and sheep. We were lucky to be in the countryside really quickly and I remembered how long it takes to drive to England's beautiful Lake District from London.

The driver entertained us with information galore, stuff about the occasional uprising, political disputes, property prices, embassy locations and peat bogs. He said a lot about peat bogs. In between, the radio music was replaced by Irish folk songs, which included one about the singer's love for a Galway Girl with black hair and blue eyes and how she broke his heart, followed by an Irish blues number which was so sad that I thought he was going to cry.

*

It was really easy to converse with my fellow back seat passenger. Happy to chat, easy flowing conversation made all the more pleasurable given that he was so easy on the eye. His gorgeous deep blue eyes distracted me from the content of his words but I doubt either of us really minded. I quite liked his combination of peaked cap, expensive new looking waterproof jacket and strategically placed frayed holes in his jeans. On someone else they may have looked scruffy but not on him, not a chance.

All the way from Colorado, USA he was on the last day of his week in Ireland and had obviously enjoyed his stay. He told me about other tours he had been on and places he had visited, what he liked and why, it was great to hear it all and consider suggestions. He seemed to enjoy telling me about his friend who visited London, met a girl, she returned to Colorado with him, stayed for a few months and now they are maintaining a long distance relationship with some success. It was a nice story, I enjoyed hearing it. I am always happy to hear about people in love.

He was a gas engineer who loves travelling but not wanting to be away from work for more than a week at a time. Although I suspect that another reason for his eagerness to be back in the States was to indulge his passion. What was his passion? He had been a skier for something like eleven years in his mountains, less than an hour from his home and now enjoys frequent snow-boarding. It seems he liked, I mean really liked extreme weather, he was used to the cold, so was not feeling our weather of the day very much at all. He was not bothered by the elements and when we complained, he was too polite to tell us to 'man up' as my children would say. Outside the bus, the cold, wind and rain made most of us glad to be inside. The frequent and thoughtful stops for photo opportunities were greeted excitedly the first couple of times but less so as the morning progressed, as fewer of us chose to leave the comfort and warmth of our vehicle.

Yes, I was on holiday and yes, I was having a great time and yes, I fully intended to enjoy myself and yes, I was happy to be there and yes, I wanted memories of my trip but no, I did not want to be cold, wet and uncomfortable. I made the executive decision to stay put in my seat. At one photo stop, my delightful back seat companion (bless him) offered me his brolly to protect myself from the rain if I wanted to leave the coach. Thanking him kindly, I explained that it was not for want of an umbrella which deterred me. Still, I could not help thinking that it was so sweet of him to offer.

Then, as if that was not sweet enough, he did something even sweeter. He left the bus at every opportunity and when he returned, he showed me the pictures he had taken. Really it was my own fault for not getting off and he did not need to go to all that trouble. What a darling. He wanted me to share and enjoy the views I was missing. Once again, I acknowledge that it was my own fault for not taking my photos. Rightly or wrongly I had made my decision and accepted the obvious consequence of no photographic evidence, not to mention the small fact of not seeing the views at all because the bus windows were totally obscured with condensation. I mean, who needs curtains when you can have condensation for free?

Earlier during the journey, the woman in front of us had draped a piece of kitchen towel roll behind her seat then waved it in front of our faces. I must not be so well versed with tour bus etiquette because seemingly I should have realised that it was being offered for window wiping. Anyway, we were glad of the paper, it was put to good use. What a day. I was already surrounded by lovely, kind, thoughtful people and there were still so much of the day left to go.

So back to my Colorado snow-boarding photographer, in gratitude for him sharing his pictures I said,

"You can be my eyes" to which he replied,

"I'm very glad to be". There was only one thought to cross my mind, I think I'm in love.

Between stops we chatted to our closest bus neighbours, a delightful couple from Lausanne, Switzerland. He was an Italian French speaking Swiss song writer, singing psychologist who had enjoyed his visits to the UK and had a particular love for London and Brighton. She was a Spanish French speaking Swiss who shared her partner's fondness for London and had Scotland high on her list of places to visit after Ireland.

I could see that the views were promising to be something spectacular and there was always a risk that I may be sorry to not have pictures as demonstration of my adventures, to share with my children and friends but my first goal was and is to be in joy. I vowed that in my pursuit of joy it would be necessary for me to stay on the bus. Besides, all was not lost for I had already decided to return to this wonderful gorgeous part of the world.

*

We stopped for lunch and not a moment too soon. I was famished. Obviously I mean that in Western terms, from a developed world perspective, as I have no personal experience of being truly starving. Anyway, I am accustomed to a fulsome breakfast of protein and starch of some description, having given up the customary choice of cereal some years ago and frankly feeling far better for it. It occurred to me one day ages ago that someone must have invented the notion of cereal for breakfast as an economics, marketing strategy because it really is not a satisfying breakfast for me and does not adequately sustain me throughout the morning. I love a bowl of muesli with fruit and nuts of an afternoon occasionally, as a snack but for brekky, no, just no.

So, as is so common when on holiday, I was out of my routine, I was hungry because I had intended to breakfast in the city before boarding my coach. What with all the morning shenanigans, it never happened. I am not very good at being hungry and after far too many hours without sustenance, I actually thought I was in danger of passing out.

Our lovely, attentive, jolly, friendly driver took us to a beautiful restaurant in a hotel which apparently has a million guests a year, according to him. My large plate of sweet rice, sweet peas, sweet carrots and salmon fillet was cooked to perfection and absolutely delicious. Table banter was comfortable and easy, sitting with the Italian Swiss guy, his Spanish Swiss friend and a delightful frequent London visitor from the Czech Republic. The Spanish lass had an enormous bowl of Guinness stew which she enjoyed so much she insisted we all try some. She was right, it was yummy. Once again I enjoyed easy flowing conversation with strangers. Well I guess it was fun talking about our travels, we shared lots of positive stories about countries we liked and loved and we were unanimous in our clear fondness for Ireland.

*

I left the group at the table to go for a wander, like you do, well I do anyway. I found a cute little shop right next door. It felt like a discovery because it was empty. With so many people in the restaurant, from our gang, another large coach party and a few car loads it made no sense that not one other customer was in the shop.

I had a quick browse. It was a cute little shop filled to overflowing with all manner of gifts. It would have been easy to spend ages in there, particularly enjoying the jokes written on many gift items. The Irish really do love their sense of humour. I decided to be sensible, as in my wanderings, I had forgotten to tell anyone where I was going. Well not so much forgotten as just did not think about it, so used am I to taking off regardless.

I browsed, selected a couple of postcards and a pretty fridge magnet with an Irish blessing. Well this was my first gift shop on my first day, I figured that I might find a few more and decided that I did not want to peak too early. The lady behind the counter looked snug and warm in her big patterned sweater and she was a real delight. She loved hearing that I was from London, that I have wanted to visit her country for---ever, that I was simply adoring her beloved Wicklow and that I was definitely planning a return visit.

After apologising for the weather, like it was indeed within her power to be responsible, I assured her that no weather could prevent me from enjoying the beauty which surrounded me. Before I left, I felt inspired to say that being also surrounded by the melodic tuneful accents of the locals was like music to my ears. I have no idea why she was surprised. Did she not realise how intoxicating her voice was? She said they take it for granted, well I guess that is not so unusual. I just told her that every time I hear an Irish person speak it is like music and that was one of the main reasons I was there.

Out of the shop and back on the bus, lucky that I did not stay and chat longer in the shop, as the bus was ready to leave and just waiting for the last member of our happy band, i.e. me. The post lunch mood on the bus was quite different. Most of us settled down for a sneaky, cheeky doze. The drive was soporific, our stomachs were full, we could not help ourselves. The spectacular view was wasted anyway due to poor visibility from the persistent condensation. Our driver substituted jolly folk songs for quiet soothing instrumentals, instead of his continual talking, he was silent, so all was quiet on the western front.

I rested my head back and closed my eyes but my head kept bobbing forward, jolting me awake to find my mouth open. Oh dear, that could not have been a good look. Glancing across at me seat companion I was relieved to see his eyes closed, so happy that he had not (or probably had not) seen me sleeping. Did I pause for a moment to watch him sleep? Well, perhaps just for a moment.

I rolled up my beautiful, soft shawl to fashion a pillow and seriously considered just popping it upon the shoulder of Mr Colorado, so as to rest my weary head, to continue my nap. However, no matter how much I thought it was a fantastic idea and no matter how convinced I was that he would not (or probably would not) have any objections, I felt that social convention dictated that it might be too soon. Following my head instead of my heart I turned towards the window and settled my head on the side of my seat.

I was happy to try to sleep though it was not easy. I was sitting beside Adonis himself. How I felt when I looked at him was under my control, that bit was easy. How I felt when he looked at me seemed to be beyond my control. When he looked at me I was totally taken in by those eyes. When he looked at me, he had all of my attention. When he looked at me, a little piece of my heart melted. Wow, the Universe was being very good to me, so many gorgeous people in such a short space of time, lucky them, lucky me. I thought it best not to imagine how different my seat companion may have been.

After seemingly ages, we stopped, the driver opened the door inviting us all to leave the bus and pointed towards a muddy path up a slope into the trees. He gleefully said it would be a beautiful walk into the countryside, affording wonderful views at the top. He promised to collect us at the other end later and prepared to drive away.

Oh really! Was he aware that it was still cold, still windy and still raining? While I was happy to be there, the prospect of trekking was not in my plans. Everyone was standing outside the bus. I stood in the doorway. I waited. I smiled. I smiled and waited. I had no objection to everyone else doing exactly what they wanted and even though clearly not everyone was thrilled at the prospect of a hike, no one said anything. They were free to choose for themselves and speak for themselves. I was concerned with my feelings and my emotions. For me, right there, right then, the suggested walk was not going to happen.

Earlier during the day, the driver had said,

"There is no such thing as bad weather, only the wrong clothing." He was right and I had no wish to argue with that. I have enjoyed, I mean thoroughly enjoyed, many a cold, wet and windy holiday in our beautiful Lake District, the Peak District, the Highlands of Scotland and our delightful North Yorkshire

Moors. Even with small children we walked up hill and down dale every day without complaint. The weather was no challenge because we were all suitably dressed with strong sturdy walking boots and performance clothing to keep us all comfortable. For this trip I decided to travel light, concentrate on shoes and dresses for dancing and keep my about town outfits to a minimum. Well, that is my excuse anyway and I am sticking with it.

So back to the muddy path idea, the driver had originally given the walk plan as a done deal, there was no suggested alternative. Perhaps, in light of our silence and lack of movement he offered an option as an afterthought. If anyone preferred to wait in the bar across the road he would return to collect from there. I needed no second bidding, immediately announcing,

"I shall be in the bar and I'll see you when you come back". I marched off without feeling inspired to wait and see if anyone else was coming. I did not feel the need to wait because... well, just because.

By myself at the counter, I ordered a pot of tea, then I turned to see another couple from the coach. Ah, so I was not the only non-trekker then. I was preparing to sit and read or write at a table by myself when the chap invited me to join them. That was kind of him. I had not interacted previously with them during the tour and I was not about to invite myself because I would not like to impose on them, so again it was nice of him to ask and I accepted the offer.

A lovely interesting couple, she was a beautiful lady wearing colourful clothing with fantastic, thick, black hair all bunched up. Interestingly, she had a propensity to throw spiritual phrases into the conversation then contradict herself by verbally demonstrating the opposite. Her partner of twelve years, tall, muscular, in leather jacket, jeans and boots, who sported a long silver pony tail, turned out to be a motor biking, social anthropologist. I confess that I do not know what a social anthropologist actually does but it sounds really cool to me.

Both from a north European capital better known for winter sports than summer holidays, I asked a question about their country, she made a comment about the cold, he suspected that she was referring to the people, she offered a response, he understood I was asking about the climate, she replied that her comment applied to both, he made a remark, she responded, he said, she said, they continued. Oh dear, I tried not to feel uncomfortable. Oh well, I know enough to understand that people create their own dynamics within relationships and what works for some may not work for others. None of it was any of my business but did help me to gain some clarity for my own perfect relationships.

With a change of subject, we light heartedly continued to chat until our driver returned after more than an hour instead of his promised twenty minutes. I have no idea what the walkers thought but it was of no consequence for us because we were warm and dry.

Back on the road, the return leg of our tour seemed to fly by really quickly. Lively chit chat resumed. My man talked about his work, about his travels setting up drilling stations and even tried to tell me where my London gas comes from. He told me who supplies Europe and what happens out of Russia and other places that did not register with me, as most of it was not really going in. Okay, he was cute but not that cute and there is only so much that even I can pretend to be interested in, before glazing over. I gently guided him away from gas, I do not remember where to, just away from gas.

Some expensive properties were pointed out including one of Bono's homes and his local watering hole leading to much discussion. The sun made a brief appearance and I ventured out for a couple of pictures of me with the bay and the coastal railway in the background. In the blink of an eye we were in Dublin city once again. We parted with lots of good byes, good wishes, smiles, hugs and hand-shakes. What happened to my cute, snow-boarding, gas engineer? He disappeared into the mist. Oh well, I am exceedingly grateful for having enjoyed such a charming companion for the day. Happiness is about the feeling in the moment, I felt great, I had enjoyed a wonderful day with wonderful people, all was well.

*

So I had ticked the top box of my 'to do' list, I had visited County Wicklow. Well done me. The only thing that mattered next was to eat.

I prided myself on easily locating the bus stop for my return journey and enjoyed watching people while I waited. Many suited city employees were making their way home and many rushed by with that look of exhaustion and preoccupation so familiar with end of weekday pedestrian traffic. I am so happy that my work is what I enjoy. I made significant changes to make it so but I still appreciate my fortunate position.

The bus journey back to my accommodation passed a Chinese take away close to my bus stop. So my dinner choice was made. Oddly it shared its premises with a pizza-burger-chippie type establishment. I say shared because there was one entrance with two separate take-aways, different counters, served by different people. Perhaps this is common in this part of the world but it was new and unusual for me.

The pizza-burger-chippie half had a selection of lively teenagers and young adults, with a group outside kicking footballs and falling from skateboards. I was not unduly concerned, I know that I am pretty tough and more than capable of taking care of myself, should the need arise. I am never one to be bothered by the exuberance of teenagers, after all, I have had the pleasure of raising two of my own. However, I felt it wise to respect the little fact that I was away from home, in another country and probably best advised to maintain some necessary awareness. Walking between the ball kicking, skate boarding youngsters, they hardly noticed me and one apologised for being in my way. How nice. All was well.

Inside, I walked past the pizza-burger-chippie counter and behind the rice and noodle counter, a lovely petite Chinese lady seemed particularly delighted to see me. No idea why but her big beaming smile was a lovely welcome. It is so nice to be warmly welcomed in a shop or a restaurant instead of being ignored as I remember so often from the past, even in local shops which I had frequented in the area where I lived for over twenty years. Many years ago, a friend and I waited by the 'please wait to be seated' sign at the entrance of a restaurant on a UK holiday, several staff passed us without acknowledging us, we could see available tables, yet we waited and waited, no seat was offered, so we left. That hurt for a long time, I wasted a lot of time and emotional energy trying to make sense of it. Now, I understand how these things work, now my experiences are so different.

Anyway, that was another time another place. Here this lovely lady insisted that I could have whatever I wanted and the chef would be happy to oblige, all I had to do was ask and it would be done. Really, anything? I considered requesting a luxury Hawaiian cruise but settled for special fried rice with extra mushrooms, as they were being so accommodating, I thought it best not to push my luck.

I had full view of the bright clean kitchen behind the sweet lady and found myself smiling at four male kitchen staff all neat in their white uniforms, black aprons and little hats. They were all staring back at me, mouths open, looking surprised or confused, I was not sure which. Thankfully when I ordered they had something to do, they sprang into action and seemed to just lose interest in gawping at me.

While I waited the lady happily talked, she seemed interested in where I was staying, why I was there, how long I would be around and what I had done that day. Then she leaned forward and beckoned me to come closer. She whispered advice to beware of the local youth as they tend to be (to use her words) "a bit cheeky!" Ah bless her, for taking care of me, for looking out for me, for being interested in my welfare. I appreciated her thoughtfulness. She need not have worried, I left and made it back down the road without incident.

Back at my room I was exhausted and ready to settle down for the night. Wait, what was this? An envelope with my name on it, in my room, on my table, what could it be? Ooh, had someone tracked me down and sent an invitation to socialise somewhere? Well almost, it was a letter from reception asking me to move out of the massive twin room which I had been moved to in error. For logistical reasons they needed me to relocate, yet again, to another teeny weeny single. I did not really care, well not much, it was no odds to me. There is always a good reason for everything and I had no idea what the Universe had in store for me that might necessitate me being in the next room, so I moved without complaint.

Room changed, food eaten I was ready to retire for the night. I had much to appreciate and be grateful for and spent some quality time counting my blessings for the many wonderful events and circumstances which I had enjoyed. I felt good. Life felt great.

*

What a wonderful way to begin my next day on holiday, I slept soundly. If there were dreams then they certainly were pleasant. So nice to wake up feeling full of energy with a keen anticipation for a new day, so nice to be convinced that amazing wonderful experiences were being lined up for me again, so nice to see how the day would unfold, so nice to wonder what circumstances and events would be brought my way to guarantee me yet another wonderful amazing time. I had been here such a short time and already had a plethora of treats.

I enjoyed a quick meditation to set my intention for the day, a quick meditation to provide and maintain the necessary grounding and balancing required before beginning any day, regardless of the agenda. No time to meditate? I make time. It is time well spent.

I had promised myself a more leisurely start to my day and at least begin with sufficient nourishment on board. My first visit to the dining room, I found the breakfast area well stocked with a long, long counter of choices. There were mini boxes of cereal, individual bowls of walnuts, sultanas, sunflower seeds, pumpkin seeds, loaves of bread, a toaster, jam, marmalade, butter, trays of sausages, bacon, eggs, tomatoes, black pudding and hash browns (or are they brownies?), as well as a selection of teas, orange juice, apple juice, bowls of apples, jugs of milk and a water dispenser. Wow, what a spread. I would be hard pushed to remember where I have seen such availability on offer for breakfast anywhere else. There was quite a choice but apart from the fruit and nuts, I was not convinced that I fancied any of it. I walked up and down a bit trying to decide.

I must have looked a little lost and confused because a guy left the table where I had seen him talking to another chap, he walked straight up to me and said,

"Are you hungry?" Looking up I saw a handsome man with short dark hair, beautiful eyes and a happy smile that lit up his face. I smiled back telling him that indeed I was very hungry, which he took as his cue to introduce me to the cauldron of piping hot porridge. Well, how clever of him to know that porridge would be the outright winner as my breakfast choice. He kindly handed me a bowl wished me a nice day, then disappeared out of the dining room. What a lovely man.

After a hearty breakfast of porridge, fruit, nuts, juice and peppermint tea, I was all set and pleasantly excited about being a proper tourist in Dublin's fair city. The other thing I was not going to repeat from the previous day was to forget to drink. I am used to drinking a lot of water throughout the day and have been a firm believer in maintaining a more than average fluid intake since a kidney function scare after my son was born.

Anyway, I digress (better get used to it, I suspect it will not be the last time). I had fully intended to eat all of my breakfast and perhaps follow it up with toast but true to form, once I had eaten what I already had, I was full. The only reason I ate the whole apple was because I was not sure how I would carry half around me to eat later.

*

Walking in the drizzle to the bus stop looking forward to making good use of day two of my bus rambler travel card, I saw the bus coming as I crossed the road. The stop was close and I could have made it if I had been inclined to speed up, or to at least break into a trot. However, there was just one teeny tiny thing that rendered that idea unworkable. I do not run. I certainly do not run for buses. I stopped running for buses years ago when I discovered that there is no need. Besides, I have said it before and I say it again, time is an illusion, so that eliminates the sense of 'waiting' for the next one.

What I fail to understand is why anyone bothers to run for a bus in London where they arrive every few minutes. There appears to be some notion of time saving or needing to hurry, both of which are fed by the false assumption that there is a shortage of time for … or … you can fill in the blanks. As my amazing daughter so rightly says "if you're not on it then it's not your train". Yeah, train or bus there is no difference, the meaning is the same.

This simple philosophy has never failed me. I have applied it to many areas of my life with outstanding results. It works. It always works. When specifically applied to buses, there has been many a time when the later rendezvous has neatly resulted in a meeting at the stop or on the bus or put me in a place and time to my advantage. Perhaps I may feel inclined to divulge more about that in another book, perhaps one about talking to strangers on buses. Anyway, I drifted off for a moment there (oops, there I go again, I did warn you).

So, there I was just a few metres away when the bus door closed and it drove away. Not the least bit concerned, I made the guided decision to walk to the previous stop and enjoy the view along the way. As if that was not enough, I felt the inclination to keep walking even further to the stop before that one. There I decided to stay put, either I did not want to push my luck or I was following my inner guidance, who knows?

Moments later I saw a little figure scuttling towards me. I looked across the path and to my delight saw the sweetest, little, old lady hurrying towards the bus stop. She approached, stood in front of me and almost like I was familiar to her, she said,

"I'm getting too old for this." Well, I could not help but laugh. Now I apologise if I am wrong here and guessing anyone's age is not a regular hobby of mine but she looked like a wonderful wise woman who had definitely lived a good number of years. Even a rough estimate is likely to be wrong, so I shall not bother. Suffice to say she was old. I had to agree with her that we are all probably too old to run for buses. She continued,

"My old mother used to say, never run after a bus or man," and with perfect comedy timing she continued, "there will always be another one along in a minute."

Well I had to laugh out loud right there in the street, as I shared her wisdom also adding, that her belief is precisely what I have passed on to my own daughter too and she neither runs after buses nor men.

Oh we did laugh, it was fun meeting her, she was a real gem. Perhaps I should not have been influenced, perhaps it should have made no difference but it was more than just her age that amused me as we shared our feminine knowing. The interaction was made more humorous on account of her sensible flat laced up shoes, calf length habit, neatly attached wimple, almost covering her wispy silver hair and her Jesus themed silver adornments. I was on holiday having fun with a sprightly elderly nun. I may be wrong but I thought I had learned over the years that nuns are not known for running after men anyway, so it was really funny to hear her quip about it.

Anyway, our interaction though brief (yet not as brief as some) would not have occurred at all if I had run for the bus in the first place or if I had stayed at one of the previous two bus stops. Seemingly, following my guidance had served me well yet again and led to more fun in the moment. Well done me.

Just as an aside, meeting this lovely lady reminded me of a lovely young lady I had the pleasure of working with in Wimbledon for a few months. We regularly shared thoughts on spirituality and enjoyed a great connection. She surprised herself by developing an affinity with nuns to the extent that she would see a few every week. Also, while travelling around South America for a couple of months, she saw one or two nuns on all of her international and domestic flights. Some might say coincidence. We thought not. We acknowledged them as representations of her angels reminding her of her constant guidance and well-being. Hey, perhaps my chance meeting with the non-bus-non-man chasing nun was an angel reminding me of something.

So back to the bus stop in Dublin, as luck would have it, we had a moment longer to chat before the bus came. I told my new nun buddy that I liked the colour scheme for the local buses, she told me they are all different but I had not seen any other colours yet. I asked whether it was necessary to actually stick your arm out and she said that they are pretty good anyway and if the drivers see you they will stop. Regular bus use in London allows for no such complacency, we know that a determined and obvious wave of at least one limb is the best course of action to avoid the risk of a bus flying past.

On the bus I considered my good fortune at enjoying such a wonderful interaction with such a delightful old person, so full of fun and being a nun with a sense of humour was a bonus. There are many ways that the meeting may not have taken place. If I had run for the first bus, if I had not walked two stops away, if I had not left my room when I did, fun with the nun would not have existed, so it is nice to know that following my inner guidance always pays and the results continue to fascinate.

*

On the bus I returned my focus to my previous thoughts of being a real proper tourist for the day. Upstairs on the double decker I enjoyed looking out of the window and noticed their emerald green post boxes were the same shape as our iconic red ones, we passed a post office painted in a matching distinctive emerald green and I saw a mail delivery chap riding a bicycle, he wore an emerald green jacket sadly the bike was not in a colour to match. More is the pity. Why did I like the colours so much? No idea I just did.

I always think it is a lot of fun to sit at the front, upstairs on a bus. I often say when at home that travelling that way is the best show in town, so it made sense to view my new surroundings from upstairs too. From my perspective I was not feeling quite like a local but I did not feel quite like a newbie either. I was beginning to recognise a few buildings, shops, businesses and roads along the way and gaining some familiarity.

From my seat I had fun eavesdropping on conversations, enjoying the occasional 'that's grand' and 'yer man' and soaking up the accents. Then my world was rocked, not a lot but rocked all the same.

A couple sat behind me and within seconds totally annihilated my romance with the much loved Irish accent. What was this? What was going on? What were they saying? I could hardly understand due to the speed and pronunciation. Initially they sounded like they were having an argument then I realised that they were just conversing. Many of the words I recognised, the manner in which they used them confused me. I do not like to be confused. Were they a Cockney equivalent? Perhaps I was being treated to some kind of Dubliana rhyming slang. The matriarch from the train sounded refined in comparison. They talked a lot, they talked fast, they talked about money and about not having enough of it, they talked about family and friends, what he said, what she said and what they said. They barely paused for breath. I thought about the lovely lady in the Wicklow gift shop and about me describing my infatuation with their melodic sweet tuneful accents. Well here I had found an exception.

My attention was soon diverted because from this same couple emanated a distracting aroma of stale alcohol and stale cigarettes. This was blended with the scent most often associated with doorway dwellers, who for their personal reasons spend their nights and sometimes days housed in cardboard and newspaper. It is a natural result of bodies and clothes that do not share frequent experiences with soap and water. The combination was enough to assault anyone's olfactory sensibilities. I had to use a focus technique which I developed for travelling on London buses when finding myself unwittingly in a similar situation. Yes of course I could just move and choose to sit elsewhere, I admit that is one obvious option. However, it is far more fun to know that I have the power to change my surroundings by changing my perspective, this way I can feel better immediately and not be dependent upon what others think, say or do. What I did was take myself mentally away from the physical reality and told myself that instead I was actually smelling strawberries, mmm... lovely, delicious, fresh, succulent, juicy, nutritious strawberries.

The mind's ability to focus is a wonderful thing and my own invented technique works a treat. I have done it many times even against the challenging whiff from a passenger who clearly has an alternative hygiene agenda for self or clothing, combined with possible issues with personal elimination control.

I recognised exactly where to get off. I was heading for the first stop of the Dublin City Tour bus. To be a real tourist I had planned to make the most of the hop on hop off tour option. I popped into a department store to avail myself of their facilities and found it pleasantly surprising. For some reason I expected it to look, well, different but it was full of shops within shops much like any department store in London. The ladies' was lovely and clean with traditional fittings and a pretty, little, wooden, upholstered sofa outside, where I parked for a moment to prepare my money for the tour bus operator.

*

I passed three red tour buses on the main road but I had already decided to give my custom to the company with the green buses, for no particular reason other than I preferred the look of them. I found a green one lurking around a corner and told the driver that I had passed some red ones on my way but had chosen his. When I asked light heartedly whether he thought I had made the right choice, he said without a hint of a smile never mind a laugh,

"Well you'll find out soon enough won't you".

I suppose I could not argue with that. I did not need him to be in a good mood for me to enjoy my day, so I remembered I was on holiday, remembered I was in Ireland, remembered I was a tourist, remembered I was there to have fun, thanked him for my ticket, smiled and made my way to the upper deck.

It was the originating stop of the tour, I was the first person on the bus, I had the choice of any seat I wanted. I decided against the open top section as it was already raining so sat at the front under cover. Moments later a group of Dutch people sat behind and across from me. They were lively, jolly and loud and obviously having a great time.

The tour was pre-recorded and the information was interspersed with folk music. Initially, I thought it was our driver talking, partly because I thought we were on a tour with live commentary, partly because I thought we were on a tour with live commentary and partly because I thought we were on a tour with live commentary. I am not saying we were misled. I realised it was a recording when everything was said in the same tone and no reference was made to anything happening in the moment.

The Dutch happy holiday makers were very entertaining it was hard not to be infected by their enthusiasm. They had an interesting way of reacting en masse to things, like every time the bus clipped the kerb (which was disturbingly frequent) they all shrieked together. Also, the commentary provided several opportunities for a collective 'ooh' 'ah' 'ouch' and 'no'. They made me laugh when the recording mentioned the wife of an important business man who had twenty one children they all shared a sharp intake of breath followed by a loud "oh no" delivered in unison as if rehearsed. To be fair I suppose the thought of twenty one children with the same mother is a little unusual.

They enjoyed the folk songs, one of them even stood up to sing along to 'Whiskey In A Jar'. He told his pals the title and when they did not believe him, he for some reason chose to include me in the conversation and asked me to confirm the song title. When I did, he was clearly delighted, his mates cheered and gave him a raucous round of applause. They did not leave him to perform on his own, oh no, they offered a tuneful rendition of 'alive alive oh' to Molly Malone, there was synchronised thigh slapping to another song, the name of which escapes me, they had a go at something like 'Glen Of The Glen', sang along to 'When Irish Eyes Are Smiling' and (bless them) knew a surprising number of words to 'Oh Danny Boy'. They were hilarious and I was surrounded, so it was just as well I enjoyed the entertainment. The tour was fun and their antics were a bonus. I jumped off the bus when the urge took me, saying good bye and thank you to the driver who chose not to respond. Oh well, never mind, I knew his well-being even if he did not.

I had no particular reason to get off the bus where I did but looked across the pavement, pleased to see that I was by the entrance of an art gallery and decided that a visit would be a great way to continue my day. I saw some attention grabbing pieces which were particularly inspiring. Lunch in the pretty sub ground floor café was a delicious hot cheesy veggie tart thing with shredded carrots, tossed in pumpkin seed, sunflower seeds and poppy seeds alongside a lettuce, rocket combo with green or runner beans, I am not sure that I know the difference. I have never been a great lover of salads so I played with the cold stuff and pushed it around the plate a bit but enjoyed the pastry dish. With a pretty glass of peppermint tea to wash it down, I was a happy bunny.

I sat there for ages writing, reading, eating slowly and being entertained by a baby in a high chair playing, the oh so successful bang-the-beaker-on-the-table game with a mother who was playing by a different set of rules. As seen so often, the difference of intention led to more than one scream from the small person when the large person attempted to terminate proceedings. The small contender was not to be defeated and demonstrated the control she had by playing the equally powerful demand-the-beaker-from-grandma-and-watch-it-fall-to-the-floor game. As frequently witnessed in this arena, grandma was well versed in the rules, dynamics and challenges of the tournament. She participated, gained proficiency and popularity, as she played along at the pace dictated by the chuckling originator.

I have a sneaking suspicion that one of the adult participants was not having nearly as much fun as I was and my thoughts were confirmed by my knowing sympathetic smile being met by looks of exasperation and eye rolling. I was enjoying myself, the baby was cute but it was time to head back as I had booked a class as the beginning of my tango weekend.

*

Proud of myself once again for finding bus stops, I made my way back to the edge of town somewhat exhausted. It is such hard work being a tourist. I fancied another lovely takeaway before my class so went to the little place that I had discovered the previous evening. Just a few young adults outside sharing cigarettes and a few inside at the pizza counter. They took little notice of me as I walked past them and to my surprise the little lady at the Chinese food counter seemed pleased, I mean really pleased to see me. I am not saying she should not have been but it was a surprise for me to see her that pleased. Anyway, I am not complaining, it is always nice to be remembered, it is always nice to be welcomed.

Such a sweetie, she asked if I wanted the same order as the previous day and I saw no reason to have something different, so I said that would be great, which seemed to excite her even more. Looking behind her the band of gents had replaced their erstwhile confused, surprised expressions with a sea of smiles. How lovely. She said that they were all happy to see me because I had come back and as I had come back, it meant that I was happy with my food and as I was happy with my food, it meant they had given me what I wanted and as they had given me what I wanted, it meant that the chef had done a good job and as the chef had done a good job, it meant that they had all made the customer happy. As if that was not enough she continued to telling me that although mine was a small order, just one dish for just a few euros, my order was as important as any other order. Oh bless them all. Who could have known that my small seemingly insignificant decision to return for another little plastic box of rice could have such an impact?

It reminds me of an independent sandwich shop I went into three times a week for a couple of months, just a few doors away from where I worked. I always went in the morning when they were quiet so no queue. I ordered the same ham and cheese in a white roll, no salad, no butter, no marge each time. Yet, every time the lady, the same lady appeared to not remember me and expressed surprise by my order. Of course this was not an issue in itself, of course I did not need her to remember me or my choice for lunch. However, when they started to give me grief over the tea, I decided it was time to stop going. Anyway, I do not need to think about them, so let us move on.

The happy-to-see-me-takeaway lady reminds me of an experience of long long ago where a work colleague who for non-specific reasons, told me that I was easily forgettable. He was convinced and more to the point found it necessary to share with me, that no one would remember me because there was nothing memorable about me. This became a belief which I bought into for many years and became one of the subjects of discussion with my counsellor for … too long.

Anyway, it does not benefit me or you to dwell upon the specifics, suffice to say he was talking from his perspective and that is nothing to do with me. That is a limiting belief that I have thankfully removed from my experience. My beliefs are quite different now and I am much the better for it. Whether I am forgettable or not is of no interest. How wonderful it is to know that from my place of freedom, I now have examples, an abundance of evidence to the contrary.

The food was delicious. After an evening of dancing my beloved tango, I went to bed at a sensible hour to maintain my energy and pace myself for the following day.

*

Saturday began with such a wonderful feeling of eager anticipation again with a joyful meditation to set my intention for the day as well as an appreciation of things past and things to come, just like I did before going to sleep. It was a fabulous night's sleep, whether due to the air, the atmosphere or both, I knew that I was loving this country, this climate, this culture, everything so far.

The previous day, I made the decision to make an early start in order to make good use of my twenty four hour hop on hop off tour bus ticket. With breakfast scheduled to begin at 8.00am I arrived at 8.04 to find the place in darkness and with no food in sight.

Back at reception the chap informed me that breakfast time had been changed for the tango group because they finish late and so breakfast was rescheduled for 10am 'til1pm instead. I thought of pointing out that I was in fact one of the tango group and in fact I finished late and I was up early and in fact fancied my breakfast but thought better of it. All I had to do was move things around a bit and return for a hearty breakfast at midday after my trip to the city. I was at the bus stop in ten minutes, the bus came immediately and I was the first passenger on it.

In the city in no time it seemed that the tour buses were not ready, I was simply too keen and too early. I went for a wander up and down the beautiful, already vibrant and buzzing O'Connell Street, past groups of excited Europeans and Americans. Something guided me to jump on a regular bus to the bridge still enjoying the use of my rambler card. I could have easily walked for it was only two stops but I took the bus and found myself outside Trinity College and there was a green tour bus.

My attempt to board was thwarted by a teeny, tiny issue. It was actually an office posing as a bus or was it a bus posing as an office, I am not sure which. Anyway, the chap at the door said that it is parked there all day to attract business, sell tickets, give information and as I soon discovered, it was also a useful base to chat up women. Not me I hasten to add, he was already holding the attention of two beautiful young lasses when I arrived. I stayed momentarily until it dawned on me that the conversation was more about their personal interest in each other and less about the tour, so I left him to it.

The real, genuine, actual, non-fake pick up point was a few metres away. I found a couple waiting there and the gentleman turned immediately upon my arrival, acknowledged me, smiled and began talking. What a lovely, friendly man. His partner was less inclined to participate, which was fine with me as he conversed easily enough for both of them. Besides, I was busy admiring her fuchsia pink glittery earrings and her profile.

There was a time back in the day, when I may have felt uncomfortable talking so freely to a man who was with a woman, who clearly did not want to join in. All sorts of feelings of insecurity would crop up, what if she thought... what if he thought... what if they thought... what if it looked like I was... blah blah blah. Thankfully I know myself well enough now, not to limit myself with such nonsense. I know my intention and that is all that matters. It is futile to concern myself with what another may or may not be thinking. Now that I know all of this, my life is so much easier.

They had just arrived in the city from the port. The sleuth in me made a deduction and asked,

"Are you on a cruise then?" He smiled saying yes, she grunted. I continued, "So where is your cruise going then?"

"Well, it's a bit of a long complicated story really", he responded.

Frankly, I failed to see how and my experience is that people who 'do cruising' like to talk about cruising so I uncharacteristically followed up with,

"Go on tell me, you know you want to."

Ha ha, there I was sounding Irish already, ah go on, go on, go on.

It transpired that he had been in Dublin just three weeks before on business and now they were both on a nine day cruise around the British Isles. How interesting to meet an English couple cruising around Britain, so not everyone races off to the tropics then. Their trip had been threatened with a force nine gale around Iona and the Mull of somewhere or other off the coast of Scotland. Also threatened with 55 mph winds off the shores of Ireland their planned route had been subject to change. This meant that this was their second stop in Dublin and were due the next day to have a second stop in Cork.

By this point our pink earring adorned lady felt inspired to join in the conversation. Turns out she was singularly unimpressed with the weather upsetting her plans, was singularly unimpressed with being in Dublin, again and singularly unimpressed by the prospect of returning to Cork, again. Was she serious? Yep. Well at least it went some way to explaining why she was not a happy bunny, as from her perspective all was not well. From my perspective I just thought, ah so you go to Cork again, big deal. You will be pleased to know that I kept my opinion to myself. The arrival of our tour bus prompted us to bid each other pleasant journeys, they sat downstairs and I sat upstairs. I could think of nothing right there at that moment in time that could persuade me to sit downstairs, so it was the upper deck for me.

*

It was Saturday, it was early the bus filled up quickly, a couple of stops later outside the beautiful Shelbourne Hotel, by the equally beautiful St Stephen's Green, a chap paused by my seat and ask if I minded him sitting beside me. Well really, why would I mind? I simply looked at him, smiled and said,

"Of course you may." Well as is so often my experience, he did not just sit, he sat and spoke. He spoke, I listened, I was happy to listen, he was cute. For the next couple of stops he amazed me by telling me that he had just flown in to Dublin that morning from Baltimore, USA. Wow, that was keen. It was not even ten o'clock and there he was on a tour already. Hey, who was I kidding, I probably would have done the same myself. Tourists do crazy things and energy seems to come from nowhere to help you fill every moment, not wanting to waste a minute or miss a thing. Unless you are an unhappy lady feeling hard done by, on a rerouted cruise around the British Isles, imprisoned by inclement weather I suppose.

Anyway, there he was fresh from Baltimore on a quick tour of Dublin intending to meet up with his brother later, the brother who lived in Lincoln, England for two and a half years and now lives in France. Wow, international travel is wonderful thing is it not? Sometimes the world seems so big and yet other times it seems so small.

I confessed that the exact location of Baltimore was unknown to me, although I do pride myself that my knowledge of US states is vastly improved, as a result of watching quiz shows and playing on line geographical games with my highly competitive son. Ooh, ooh and let us not forget that my working knowledge of US states was complimented by my back seat Wicklow tour companion. Our shared pointing and gesticulating on the imaginary map of North America on the back of the seat in front was evidently time well spent. So from Mr Colorado to Mr Baltimore, focus Carole focus. With his short brown hair, handsome face, warm eyes and friendly smile, he seemed happy to explain that Baltimore is just south of Washington not in the middle but on the east coast. Well now I am even wiser. We shared our joy of the day's fine weather and I nearly told him that the sunshine yellow, waterproof, walking jacket that he was wearing was enough to brighten even the dullest of days but thought better of it and once again decided to keep my opinion to myself.

The recorded commentary was okay, I was having fun and enjoying the company but felt the urge to leave the bus a few minutes later. I had no particular reason it was just an urge so I followed it. As always I said thank you to the driver, meaning to jump off but somehow his soft sweet delicious Irish accent expertly and easily engaged me in conversation.

How is it that so many people can sound so genuinely interested in me in such a short space of time? Hey, I really do not know. Perhaps they are not really interested at all but they sound it and that is good enough for me, or perhaps I should say 'that's grand'. Anyway, I have known people for thirty years who are not the least bit interested but as they are no longer essential to my experience I can let them go.

Anyway, I digress once again. I offer no apology because the digressions such as they are, contribute towards the ingredients of my story soup. So back to the driver, who had my attention with a "where are you from" and a "where are you going" and a "where have you been" and a "where are you staying" and more. Turned out he liked London, had a friend who lived in the centre, Waterloo to be precise, I agreed that Waterloo is indeed pretty central. After learning I am from south London he mentioned another friend who lived in Highgate. My response was to say (although I did not realise it at the time) somewhat dismissively "oh that is North", which for some reason reduced him to hysterics. He was amused because apparently Dubliners have the same city north south distinction, with the general recognition that they are quite different. So something else I had learned. He finished with "you're in the North now" and I jumped off waving a fond farewell to my new friend.

What a wonderful friendly interaction that was. He seemed unconcerned that his full bus was waiting. Perhaps they were equally unconcerned that the driver was enjoying a quick chin wag. It was all good.

*

I found myself on a street where I had been before, so I recognised where I was and impulsively decided to pop into the tourist office. I had no particular reason, I did not know why I was going in, I just felt the urge so I followed it. It was huge, easily ten times the size of the one where I booked and rebooked (don't remind me) my Wicklow day out. This was not some little shop with a couple of racks of leaflets, a few posters and a handful of gift ideas. Oh no, this was much more. With numerous carousels, shelves, racks and cabinets, this place offered all manner of memorabilia with an entire area dedicated to visiting suggestions and another section for accommodation bookings. I could see that I was in danger of being spoilt for choice, so I settled for a pretty key ring. With so many lovely things to choose from and more days of my holiday left, once again, I did not want to peak too early.

This may be a good opportunity to take a moment to briefly mention grammatical accuracy. I know that it is more correct to say 'with so many lovely things from which to choose...' but who actually speaks like that? I mention it because if by some fluke my children were to read this account of my tales, I suspect they would both be mortified by any tendency to end phrases and sentences with a preposition. I may be guilty as charged and I adore that they are both pedants (please do not get either of them started on the use and abuse of the apostrophe) but my excuse is that I am writing as the mood takes me in the moment.

Carole Chandler

I wandered to the counter, in no particular hurry still browsing, noticing the Gaelic inspired jewellery, humorous socks and framed artwork. I found myself behind a well-dressed lady with blond and silver hair, wearing a navy quilted jacket, hovering in front of the payment counter. She seemed to be looking around, so I was unsure whether she was waiting to pay or not. Like I said I was no particular hurry, so I waited until she looked in my direction. I smiled and asked whether she was waiting. When she said yes but it was okay if I wanted to go first, I replied,

"That's fine, I didn't know whether you were waiting but if you are the queue then I'm more than happy to wait behind you."

She beamed and said, "Ooh, an English voice, how lovely."

I laughed and said, "Oh, I don't know, I'm enjoying being surrounded by Irish accents while I'm here."

She agreed and we briefly compared holiday notes about the fun time we were having and how adorable the people were and how easy it was to get about.

We enjoyed a lovely chit chat, she was in Dublin with her husband who was off doing his thing that day, whatever his thing was. She was having such a good time, that she was considering returning on her own, especially as her spouse disappears a couple of times a year to play golf with his pals. She seemed to light up when she told me that she was toying with the idea of revisiting the museums and 'doing some sketching'.

I happily shared with her that I was in the city on my own, enjoying being a tourist and taking part in an Argentine Tango weekend festival. She thought that was lovely and although she did not tango she liked line dancing. I suggested that there was probably line dancing available somewhere in

Dublin and she thanked me for the idea. We will never know where that conversation may have led her. For all we know she is travelling the world winning line dancing competitions as a result of our brief interaction.

*

So what was next? Ah yes, it was time to hop on another tour bus. Well, I am sincerely glad that I did, it was the highlight of my day. No really, it was. The next green tour bus that came along was not nearly as busy as the one where I had just left Mr Baltimore. I hopped on, said hallo to the driver who glanced at my ticket, which meant I did not need to pay again. He waved me through with a,

"Hallo there, how are ya?"

I went straight upstairs and chose to sit towards the back, out in the open this time as the clouds were less abundant, the sun was making intermittent appearances and instead of cold, wet and windy at least it was just cold and windy so things were looking up.

We set off and then the rarest of treats began. The driver spoke. Yes, the actual driver spoke to the passengers. He spoke to us in real time. It was not a recording, not a distant commentary. I would never have guessed that it could make quite such a difference. Well, to me it did and for me it was a demonstration of the power of being in the present moment. Seriously, it is one of the aspects of any interaction that really, truly and honestly makes a difference. Admittedly a recording conveys the historical information but as experiences go, the live commentary puts the tour in a completely different league.

The moment that made me sit bolt upright and pay attention was when I heard,

"Good mawnin', moy name is ..."

He proceeded to say his name in the most musical melodic way I have ever heard a name spoken. He dragged out the first syllable with such a long protracted vowel sound that I wondered if he had spent ages practising and recording himself, to listen to how his name sounds in a variety of ways before deciding on the optimum pronunciation. He followed up with,

"And oy am yer droyva fer yer tour today."

What I am endeavouring to demonstrate here, is his delicious Irish accent, though not easy to write down and really needs to be heard to be savoured. Perhaps you will be lucky enough, one day, to rendezvous with him and his bus and hear him for yourself but until then I shall continue.

He was one of the funniest men I have ever had the pleasure of hearing. I have enjoyed many a stand-up comedian on television, on the radio and have even paid money to see some live on stage. This chap was as good as any of them. As with the style of so many comedians, his material was mostly on the wrong side of political correctness but that did not stop us all laughing with delight. The only issue it caused me was when I found myself raving about him later to some of the dance crowd, I was asked to share some of his jokes. Most of his material consisted of strings of snappy, quick fired one-liners, so hard to remember anyway. I decided that I was not willing to repeat the funniest one which I could easily recall, due to its shock value component in the lead up to the funny ending. Besides, I would not have been able to do it justice so the humour would have been lost anyway.

The actual jokes were not the point, what mattered was how I felt and how funny it was to hear him deliver his material. He gave information about the sights just as in the recordings and spiced up the trip with his own jokes and witty stories, he was relentless, he was hilarious. When our driver was not educating us with dates and facts about buildings and statues, he was telling us about his ex-wife, mother-in-law, places he had been and things he had done. The man must have been born to bring humour, to make people laugh and he did it really well. Prior to boarding I had planned to only stay on the bus for a few stops but after hearing him, there was no way I was going to leave early, I did not want to miss any of his performance so I stayed for over an hour. It was worth every moment.

Part of the fun was the way he commented on people and places that we passed, which were clearly not part of the official tour. As we passed the Guinness museum he spotted a couple of beautiful young ladies walking by. Obviously a little distracted he stopped the bus to call out to them,

"Hallo beautiful, d'ya have a boyfriend?"

I found it amusing that he spoke to both of them together and one of chose to answer having decided that he was talking to her I suppose. Well good for her. Her affirmative response was no deterrent as he followed up with,

"Would ya like another one?" It was harmless, they laughed and we laughed.

Later he excused himself while he listened to a message from his office, concerning some lost property on the bus then asked us to let him know if anyone found the missing bag. He drove on, he talked, we laughed, he talked some more, we laughed some more. A few minutes later he stopped the bus, turned off the engine and apologised for the interruption. He was following instructions from the office to personally check for the lost property upstairs.

Carole Chandler

I saw him come up and look around so I took the opportunity to speak to him when he approached my seat. I felt the impulse to just say how funny I thought he was and how much I was enjoying the tour. He stopped, looked at me, smiled, sat down beside me and shouted to the whole bus,

"We're not going anywhere for a while folks, I'm staying here with my girlfriend."

With that, he put his arm around my shoulders and pulled me towards him. Ah, how lovely, I received a hug from our driving jester. I knew he was harmless, I knew he was just doing it for laughs (or for funzies as my daughter says, or for j-okes as my son says), he was all about the humour. Though I think it is probably fair to say that it is not difficult to fall in love with someone who makes you laugh like that. Moments later he disappeared back downstairs.

The tour continued with as much laughter and hilarity as before. Sadly, as with all good things, it had to come to an end. I did not want to leave but the tour was obviously going to come to a natural end at some point anyway. On leaving the much enjoyed moving comedy zone, I followed the impulse to give our talented funny man a fat tip, which was merely a representation of the joy he brought. It was worth it. I thanked him for the last time and he surprised me by saying,

"You're lush you are."

Ah, how sweet. Have I ever been called lush before? Not that I can remember.

*

I left the bus feeling 'top o' the mawnin', well I think that is what it feels like, I know I felt fantastic anyway. Wandered down a busy pedestrianized shopping street, enjoying the beautiful selection of shops, much like many streets in London, to be sure, to be sure, then decided to pop into the St Stephen's shopping centre. It had been mentioned on all of the tours and I liked the look of the exterior with its glass and curves. I fancied a look inside and found it to be quite a treat and unlike any other shopping centre I have seen.

It was a shopping mall but looked small and cosy rather than large and rambling. The shop fronts seemed quaint in shape and design. The network of stairs, escalators and walkways gave it a fun-fair roller coaster type of feel. Of course, I am not referring to the speed of anyone or anything and I heard no screams for the atmosphere was actually quite relaxed. I refer merely to my impression and perspective in the moment. It was cute and I loved it. I would have liked to visit St Stephen's Green too but decided to save it for another day as I had other things to do before heading back for my late breakfast and tango lesson.

I strolled back down the street past the rows of shops again. It was busy with a continuous flow of people walking in both directions down both sides, in and out of the many shops and cafés. A lady called out to me, I paused, I looked, she shouted,

"Hallo, hallo, ya'll stop, ya'll stop won't ya darlin', I know ya'll stop and talk to me, oy know ya will, oy know because ya got a nice face, ya got a kind face and oy know Jesus loves ya."

Well I could not really argue with any of that and did not even consider walking away, I mean really, what harm could come of it? So I allowed her to continue. She said,

"Do ya have a minute to listen to me darlin', do ya?"

I did not say no, I looked at her, I smiled, I did not say anything, I tried not to focus on her appearance and as I had not specifically told her to buzz off, she seemed to settle and began talking.

Her introduction was about the trolley she trawled behind her which she informed me contained the clothes of her seven children, who needed food. She had left her husband because she did not like his behaviour, she was hungry and they were hungry. She spoke quickly, very quickly, hardly pausing for breath. I listened. She asked if I would just give her some money to buy food, or would I just give her some money, or would I just buy her something to eat, or would I just buy her a burger.

Well as luck would have it, we were indeed conveniently located right by the entrance of a well-known burger-in-a-bun emporium. Unlucky for her, I had no intention of going into that one or another any time soon. That was not an option. I did not have any money handy and I did not feel inspired to take my purse out of my bag and start looking for money particularly in an unfamiliar place with unfamiliar people around. I like to think well of others but I like to be aware too. However, I had listened, I was happy to help and I had an idea.

She stopped talking. I paused and told her that I had a croissant in my bag, which she was quite welcome to have. It was true, I had bought two earlier in the day and had eaten one on the bus, while being amused by our funny man jester driver. Initially my offer was met with disdain, as she thought I had said that I had a cross in my bag. To avert further confusion I described the croissant as a roll, a bun, a pastry, well something to eat anyway.

"You can have the croissant if you are hungry."

"What about if ya just buy me a burger?"

"You can have the croissant if you are hungry."

"Would you just give me some money to buy a burger?"

"You can have the croissant if you are hungry."

"What about the children?"

"You can have the croissant to eat now if you are hungry, I'll give it to you now, you can have it now."

We seemed to reach an impasse. She snarled, glared and said something indiscernible, threw her arms into the air, stamped her feet, grabbed the handle of her trolley and stomped away.

Well there you have it. I was left hanging. A stranger asked me for food. I offered her food. She exercised her right to decline. I am not saying she was ungrateful, I could not possible know the inner workings of her mind but what I do know is that it was another brief encounter.

*

Apart from her reaction, meeting this lady was not so unusual. I am frequently stopped and asked for money. I almost always listen. What I never do is allow myself to be swept up by their story. I do not allow it because it does not benefit them and it does not benefit me. Sometimes I feel inspired to hand over cash and sometimes I do not. A surprising number of times when I have not given money, they have thanked me for stopping and thanked me for listening. So often someone feels the need to be heard. I know what that is all about, to feel unseen and unheard, that was a cross I carried for many years.

My snarling, glaring, perhaps not-so-hungry-after-all lady reminded me of an evening once in Covent Garden, London when I had bought a tub of mushroom soup on my way to a meeting. For one reason or another I did not eat it, so a couple of hours later I found myself carrying it home, when I passed a chap sitting in a shop doorway surrounded by cardboard, who appeared to be settling down for the night. It occurred to me that I was considering carrying a cold cup of soup all the way home to heat up and eat the next day. Did I really want to do that? In reality I probably would have disposed of it anyway. I retraced my steps and offered it to the doorway man.

"Ooh, thank you," he said excitedly.

I told him it was cold, he said it really did not matter, he did not mind at all. I told him it was mushroom and I hoped that was okay and I remember him saying,

"Mmm... that's my favourite". He shouted thank you again, called me a kind lady and waved as I walked away.

Then there was the young snotty guy who appeared seemingly out of nowhere at a bus stop in Merton High Street, south west London, asking me (very politely I might add) for twenty pence. I looked in my pocket and it was empty. He thanked me for looking. Inspiration took hold of me as I looked at his face. I did not need to know his story but something made me ask,

"How much do you need?" He said,

"Well, I really need a pound but I don't like to ask for too much." Without hesitation I gave him a pound coin from my purse. His face lit up, he thanked me repeatedly, grabbed my hand and kissed it. When he moved towards me to kiss my cheek, I realised that while I was happy that he was happy, the snotty face was reason enough to maintain a respectful, healthy distance. I assured him that further demonstrations of gratitude were not required. He thanked me again, called me a beautiful angel and disappeared.

I have recently followed the inspiration to carry change with me to give to people when the mood takes me. I just love the joy it seems to give them in receiving a handful of coins. It makes my purse lighter as well as my heart, so everyone wins. So you see, the food refusing trolley lady had little impact on me, she was just doing exactly what she wanted and I shall continue to do what I want.

*

I still had my croissant and fancied a hot drink and noticed several places with drinks machines for tea, coffee and hot chocolate to take away. I have seen those here in petrol stations but never in ordinary shops. I think it is a great idea.

The shop I felt inspired to go into had no cups in the dispenser, so the lovely smiling gentleman behind the counter asked someone out the back to remedy the situation. A small woman arrived with a huge, dense, metaphorical, black cloud hanging right over her, as she brought a packet of disposable drinks containers. All the while she complained about the staff, the shop, her life and how she was planning to run away and leave everybody. She declared for the whole shop to hear that she was sick of all of them and that she had had enough. I looked at the man and said nothing. He said,

"She's a complainer, she always complains." Looking back at her, I believed him, her furrowed brow and major air of despondency looked permanent. I looked back at him and said,

"Yes, I can see that, well she won't be like it for much longer, she'll work herself into an early grave." I have no idea what possessed me to say that, I do not remember using those words to or about a stranger before but it just slipped out. It was too late, what was said was said. In response he laughed and agreed. Yes, that is right, he laughed and agreed.

I turned back to the seriously disgruntled lady who continued to openly share her woes with no one in particular. She had her back to me, I moved towards her, I put my hand on her shoulder. She stopped talking, turned her head and looked at me. I smiled, her face softened, I felt tension release in her upper body as her shoulders dropped. After a pause I said,

"You'll be fine, everything will be alright". She continued to look at me, I reiterated, "you'll be fine".

I will not say that she smiled because she did not, clearly that would have been far too big an emotional jump from where she was currently holding her focus but she definitely softened and said quietly, "I hope so."

To give hope where hope is needed is a job well done.

*

My next quest was to find somewhere to drink my hot chocolate and eat my erstwhile rejected croissant. Heading towards Trinity College, the pavements were busy and a charity clipboard chap called out to me through the crowd. Yes, yes, yes I know the current affectionate term for them is 'chuggers' but that does not resonate with me. Well, you should have seen him, how could I not respond? His handsome face, short brown spiky hair, trim physique, neat clothes and beautiful bright eyes were enough to persuade me to dreamily follow his call. He had a chin stubble thing going on, which enhanced his appearance and coming from someone who prefers the clean shaven look, that is saying something. Little did he know that he already had my attention, before he asked if I could spare a minute to hear about his chosen charity. While he spoke, I began to lose myself, as I gazed into the deep, blue windows of his soul. I was sinking deeper and deeper, I just knew that it would have been bliss indeed to hear more of his delicious Irish accent but...

As if flicking a switch, I regained my focus, broke his spell and remembered my quest. I told him that I did have time to listen and would love to hear more but really needed to have my drink and something to eat, so he kindly directed me towards the college café. I was heading towards the grounds anyway but it was interesting to learn from him that it would be acceptable to take my own food into their café.

I walked through the entrance to the college and oh my goodness, I had not expected such beauty. Looking around enjoying the resplendence, I reminded myself to close my mouth. Wow, the buildings and landscaping were so gorgeous. There were groups of people in every direction, lots of people enjoying the gardens. Clearly this was a popular place for tourists.

As I enjoyed the grounds I was walking across the open square, when I became aware of a person moving at a pace diagonally across the square, walking purposefully towards me. He was clear in my peripheral vision. Hey, I am not implying that he made a bee line for me but, well, he made a bee line for me.

I looked in his direction and he continued to approach at speed, when from a few metres away he called out,

"Cold isn't it?" I agreed, well it was hard not to, as the blustery wind in this open space made it feel even colder. What a big smile he had, a big beaming smile like the Cheshire Cat himself. He certainly seemed happy about something or perhaps someone.

He apologised for the weather telling me that it is normally warmer at this time of year. Once again the Irish accent had my attention, his dark suit, modest tie, pink and white striped shirt and leather shoes, did not go unnoticed either. If there is one thing I have always had a preference for, it is a man in a suit. Anyway, I wondered briefly about the propensity for the Irish people I had met to apologise for the weather. At no time had I held any person individually or collectively responsible for the cold, the wind or the rain. I know that the English like to talk about the weather but I have never heard anyone personally apologise for it. Following his apology for the weather I may have said something, perhaps a few words along the lines of being grateful that at least it was dry and not raining as it had since my arrival. Also, I may have said something about loving the city, having a great time and thinking of returning. He was a local, was glad that I was enjoying my holiday, introduced himself and when I told him my name he held my hand with both of his hands for a long firm hand shake. Interestingly, he held my hand for longer than is customary given the brevity of our acquaintance.

"So where ya from then Carole, where ya from?" He seemed happy to hear that I am from London and seemed even happier to tell me that he visited London six years ago and really liked it.

"So do ya like to travel then Carole, do ya, do ya like to travel?" I told him that I do indeed and I have travelled a lot.

"So where do ya like to travel then Carole, where do ya like to travel?" I replied that I have been to many places but I really like cities, I like the buzz of lots of people.

"So do ya like cruising Carole, do ya, do ya like cruising?" I informed him that although I have never been on a cruise, it sounds like fun and is on my list of things to try. I briefly mentioned the people I had met that morning who were having mixed experiences on their cruise around Britain. I was happy to hear him talk about a cruise he took last year around the Caribbean islands for ten days, after his flight to the US to join the cruise ship and how nice he found the weather and the people.

"I'm single and I love to travel. Are ya single Carole, are ya, are ya single?" I thought nothing of it, just enjoying our friendly chat on this lovely day, in this friendly city, in this lovely location. I spontaneously responded with how great it is to be single and enjoy the freedom of being able to take off whenever I choose.

"So where are ya staying then Carole, where are ya staying?" Well I had been asked that question frequently during my short time in the city from a whole variety of people in my wanderings, so I felt no reason to be concerned.

When I told him the name of the district he looked a little confused and asked why I was staying so far from the centre. It seemed only natural to mention the Argentine Tango festival because it was the reason that I was staying in that particular location.

"So do ya like to dance then Carole do ya, do ya like to dance?" I said how much I enjoy it and that the weekend was fun with classes and general dancing for the whole weekend. He told me that he likes to dance too, which I thought was nice.

"So do ya have a dance partner then Carole do ya, do ya have a dance partner?" Whenever I talk to new people about my dance passion, they always ask this question, so I just told him what I tell them, that I do not have a specific partner, I just dance with whoever is there at the venue at the time. We talked and talked right there in the square, he asked questions, I answered, he told me about himself, he asked me about myself.

This may be a good time to point out that during our easy, flowing conversation I had considered it merely light hearted friendly communication. I was singularly unconcerned by the dialogue and only slightly distracted by his conversational style of repeating himself, repeating himself, particularly his questions, particularly his questions and using my name a lot and using my name a lot.

I do not know how it happened (really I do not) but somehow he asked me about the venue, the location, how to get there, the times of the social dancing and I had already answered. Somehow, it was not until he told me that he was intending to show up in the evening at the dance to enjoy having some dances with me, not until then did alarm bells start to ring. Boy did they ring. Ouch, what was I thinking? Really, what was I thinking?

Please do not misunderstand me, I am open to opportunities. I am willing to allow the Universe to drop an unattached, tall, strawberry blonde, blue eyed, chatty, deliciously accented, suit wearing, cruise loving, dancing, international traveller into my lap. I am more than willing, except for one teeny tiny thing, this particular gentleman was not on my list. Why? Just because he did not press my buttons and that is all there is to it. Suffice to say I made my excuses and left.

On reflection it may be easy to think that it was a close shave but not really. I mean at no time was I in any actual danger. I guess he was harmless enough. I am happy to carry on thinking that he was a sweet, charming guy looking for someone to be sweet and charming with. I have since discovered that others may not agree with me. I told a friend about the incident and he was overly amused when I told him about the conversation and laughed telling me that I was not being 'chatted to', I was being 'chatted up'. Well I did not think so. He called me naïve. Well I do not think so. I told my daughter. She was unimpressed by my interpretation of the college gardens man's line of enquiry.

"You really should be more aware mother!"

I failed to see why and I failed to see what difference it would make.

"You should know when you're being chatted up."

I still failed to see why and I still failed to see what difference it would make.

Time to move on.

*

I continued to walk towards the exit of the college grounds, still amused by the events which had just transpired. I was grateful for the pleasant interaction and acknowledged how many boxes he did tick, so happy in my awareness and appreciation of that.

A couple stopped me before I reached the gate, the gentleman asked me if I would take a photograph of them and handed me his camera. Why do I mention this? Simply because it happens often and it never ceases to amaze me when it does. With so many people milling around, they chose to ask me. In a busy place with hundreds of tourists, they selected me. Some might say coincidence, I think not.

Another trip on a local bus saw me back safe and sound. My late breakfast was an excellent substitute for lunch and after my eventful morning I needed the nourishment. I eventually located the tango crowd as everyone had been moved to an alternative room. Helped myself to a few bits from the selection and glanced around the room. A couple of people here, a few people there, no one in particular caught my eye, so I walked to the other side of the room to a couple of ladies at a table with lots of spare seats. I smiled, asked if I could join them and sat down. That was it. They spoke in English and another European language for the rest of the time, without acknowledging me further. Oh well, can't win 'em all I suppose. I had no intention of intruding in their conversation or imposing, so I sat in silence. I know that I could have moved and sat elsewhere but I was not bothered enough to find other companions. It gave me an opportunity to make notes for this book and with so many events to make notes about, from that morning's experiences alone, I leisurely ate my meal and made good use of the time without interruption.

After my tango lesson I jumped on a bus and took off into town again. I really wanted to make the most of my holiday and was determined to get a good grasp of this being a tourist lark. I could have stayed at the venue and mingled, making small talk with fellow tango lovers but I figured there was plenty enough time for that. Besides, (and this is the fact that some others failed to appreciate) I was in Dublin to be in Ireland and the tango was a bonus, whereas the others were there for the tango which just happened to be in Ireland. Anyway, clearly I was feeling uber confident that I could make it to the city and back in an hour. Clearly I trusted that the bus service would not let me down. Clearly I believed that I would not get lost in the process.

The city was heaving. Oh and by the way, why were there men wearing kilts and why was a man on a street corner playing bagpipes? While I had my wits about me to (eventually) fend off the aforementioned dancing cruiser, I also found the courage, (although I did not think so at the time) to walk into a restaurant after a cursory glance at the menu outside. Like everywhere else I had passed, it was packed but unlike the other places which I had passed, I did not know that this one was packed because I could not see inside. I just walked in. On reflection I must have been insane to even consider sitting in a packed restaurant in the city on a Saturday afternoon all by myself. Well I was not really thinking was I? The magic of Ireland had obviously gone to my head and made me do things totally out of character.

It was beautifully decorated in red and yellow with dark wood. The staff looked pretty busy but I walked up to the counter and enquired boldly,

"Do you have a table for one?"

 116

I still have no idea what came over me. Who was this new woman? Where was this newly discovered carefree personality coming from? I hardly recognised her. I liked her. Anyway, I sat at a table then saw that the menu was tapas. I told you it was a cursory glance outside, so I had not looked properly. I decided that this place was not appropriate for me at that time, made my excuses and left. So what did I learn from that experience? I learned that I can walk into busy restaurant in an unfamiliar city with the happy intention of sitting and eating alone. It was great. I felt great. I felt like I could do anything. I know that I did not actually do it but I was going to, so there.

Deciding not to test my bravery skills further, I liked the appearance of a pretty, little, rustic looking café, popped in, bought a mini ricotta and spinach quiche, as well as a plum and almond muffin. They turned out to be excellent choices indeed. Back at the common room, my quiche was delicious and not in the least bit ruined by being heated in a microwave. The muffin, due to its humongous size and filling yumminess lasted two days. I was in no hurry to eat it all at once and had the pleasure of enjoying it in stages.

*

My second tango class for the day was yet another welcome opportunity to chat to strangers. Now then, I have been dancing a variety of dances for a number of years. When it comes to talking to strangers on the dance floor I have experiences to fill many books, however, I made the decision not to let this one be about the dancing. Considering that tango was one of the reasons for my visit, a few snippets would be unavoidable.

The classes were great fun and we changed partners often, giving us the opportunity to meet new people. Dancing can be an emotional activity, Argentine tango is particularly intense at the best and worst of times and while I could say much more about how and why, I feel that this is not the right time or place to start going into it.

Earlier I said that dancing can be an emotional activity. Correction, dancing is a very emotional activity. Whether good or bad I suspect it is hard to be indifferent about it. I think it is probably fair to say that dancing changed my life. Without it I may never have experienced the feeling of happiness. Before I learned to dance, how I felt every day was just how I felt every day. The overwhelming sensations of joy experienced on the dance floor were new to me and I liked the feeling, I liked it a lot. I danced often to feel better but I did not realise why I felt better, more to the point I did not realise why it mattered. The Carole on the dance floor was a completely different person to the Carole everywhere else. This was unsustainable, something had to give.

The specifics are inconsequential and dwelling on details would be of no benefit to you and certainly of no benefit to me. I have learned that all it does is hold us all in that negative place and subsequently compromises our ability to improve situations. Anyway, my story is different now. I am sure you have your own and can fill in your own blanks. Thankfully I discovered and understood very quickly the power of feeling good now. Obviously not at the beginning but somewhere along my journey, I made the decision to take a break from my beloved dancing to concentrate on modifying, changing and improving the aspects of my life which were not pleasing to me.

Now I am back. I used to dance to feel happy, now I dance because I am happy.

I had fun before but now my jive, salsa and tango are incredible. Every dance is a wonderful dance and every leader is a wonderful leader. I feel no need to pretend that they are, they just are. That is how life is now. That is my perspective now. The best thing about everything I have learned is the knowledge that everyone, absolutely everyone has the power to feel this way, if they wish to and if they choose not to, then that is okay too.

Just a tad side tracked there. So I was dancing at the tango festival...

*

A guy made me laugh out loud unintentionally as he tried a new technique. He talked himself through the sequence and said,

"So, I change my weight and step forwards towards my opponent."

His opponent? Really? Come on now, that is hilarious. How could I not laugh? I guess his malapropism gave me some idea of how he felt about his tango, his role as a dance leader and about his inner turmoil. He apologised and passed it off as something to do with mixing his words up with his other hobby of fencing. I did not buy it. I know how tango affects us. Inner turmoil sounded far more plausible. Once again I kept my opinions to myself, he did not need my input and seemed to feel bad enough already.

Soon I was dancing with another new leader, a German living in Dublin. He expressed amusement about the fact that so many people had come to the event from all over Europe and as he lived in the capital, it was a convenient location for him. Maybe something has been lost in the translation but he seemed tickled by it anyway.

Soon I was dancing with another new leader, a Tunisian living in France, a powerful leader with a wonderful dynamic flourish to his moves. The fact that he danced in bare feet did not distract me, well not much. His crop of stunning, dark brown, curly hair was really beautiful and I somehow managed to restrain myself from running my fingers through it. I was tempted though and I have many a time found myself dancing and playing with a leader's hair when it is long and lovely. I know a few tangueros with shoulder length locks and they have voiced no objections to me stroking their hair while we move around the floor.

Soon I was dancing with another new leader, a chap wearing a humorous, hard to ignore t-shirt, purchased in Dublin, with a slogan further expressing the notion that the Irish are fond of a drink or two. Mind you there is little point me objecting on their behalf, as they say it often enough themselves. The performance by the tour bus, funny man jester driver chappie is a case in point. He made many a reference to the nation's imbibing habits.

Soon I was dancing with another new leader, a quiet chap, a very quiet chap who did not make eye contact once and said not a single word, not one.

Soon I was dancing with another new leader, an intense well built, broad shouldered gent in the regular uniform of black trousers and black t-shirt, a combination so often favoured by male dancers. I have heard guys have an entire conversation extolling the virtues of the black t-shirt / black trousers combo, stating it as the optimum choice for boys on the dance floor. This chap was intense indeed. The new technique we were learning together was not going well from his point of view, I was happy enough. He wanted it to be better, I was happy enough. He wanted me change what I was doing. I knew that what I was doing worked pretty well with the others but I chose not to mention it. Guys generally do not respond well to that kind of input. He actually said he wanted to discuss what was 'going wrong'. I was not going to let him catch me out like that. I have been there before and I do not go there anymore.

It would have been necessary for me to come out of my happy, good feeling emotional place to pick the bones out of it like he wanted to. From my perspective all was well, I was happy. From my point of view there was nothing to discuss. I stayed with my perspective and allowed him to stay with his, I smiled sweetly and as luck would have it, soon I was dancing with another new leader.

*

It was time for dinner. The event organiser had arranged for the on-site restaurant to open for dinner just for us on the Saturday night, so I looked forward to taking advantage of that. Of course it was also an opportunity to have fun meeting more dancers. With my tray of salmon fillet, swede, carrots and potatoes, I approached a table with two ladies and lots of spare seats. In response to my "may I join you" they both immediately said hallo, gestured to the seat and introduced themselves. What a contrast to my breakfast/lunch experience. Like I said then, you can't win 'em all, well this time I won.

We spent well over an hour engaged in lively friendly banter which entertained us all. They were two beautiful French ladies living in Paris and both spoke English, which I am grateful for because my French would not have been sufficient to hold a conversation with them. One of the ladies was more confident than the other, so much of the conversation consisted of French being spoken between them, one telling me what the other meant, me saying something in response, then my meaning being relayed to the other. Either way it was fun and caused much laughter with the bonus of improving my French enormously.

A gentleman they had met in an earlier class joined us. He was originally from London and living in Belfast for the past few years. He had already eaten but was keen to talk to the girls about something preying on his mind. Poor love, he was agonising over the content of a class which they had taken on musicality and tormented himself with his own notes on a scrap of paper. Oh dear, it all looked very complicated with scribbled numbers, arrows and boxes. I could not help thinking that it did not look like fun at all.

He was determined to make some sense of it. The girls teased him, they had met him before. He sat opposite me, I listened. He stressed and stressed, his anxiety increased. I suspected that there had to be another way. I put my hand on his hand, I said his name, he stopped talking and looked at me. I took his piece of paper and turned it over, the reverse was blank, so there was no writing to fret about.

I said, "There you are."

He smiled and said, "That's better, I don't feel stressed now."

The girls laughed, the one beside me looked at me and I leaned over and said,

"That is what I do. I told you I relax people." How nice of her to say that I am good at it. I asked our now non stressed man whether he was a scientist or mathematician or perhaps an engineer. He confirmed that his profession calls for mathematical analytical skills on a regular basis. I said softly,

"This is tango, don't analyse, feel the music."

My work was done. He was happy, well at least happier. In his revised frame of mind he stayed for a while. Once or twice the conversation veered dangerously close to politics and I managed to steer it back to something lighter before we became embroiled. We were only a small group so this was possible. In larger gatherings I have learned to keep my mouth shut and focus my mind during discussions of less positive matters. He wanted to know why I preferred to be positive. I said I was being me. He said,

"All of this p.c. zen stuff is all well and good but what about when a real issue needs to be discussed, you can't just say everything is okay."

I felt secure enough to tell him that I could say that. He was not satisfied,

"What if someone's leg is hanging off, you can't just put it to one side and say, there, there, it'll be fine, can you?"

I replied, "Yes I can, pretty much."

He announced he had something to do and left. So, there we were back to our previous dynamics of me and the two French girls. Somehow we stumbled across the less often visited subject of my stressful job prior to my present stress free occupation. I had no idea how much they knew or understood about hospitals and nursing especially neonatal nursing, so I kept it simple. It transpired that they really understood because they were both, wait for it ... they were both paediatricians.

Well the proverbial feather could have knocked me right off my seat. Here was I thinking that I was passing the time with a couple of young, care free lasses about town and they turn out to be qualified medical practitioners, already in their specialist fields no less. I guess now would be a good time to stop calling them girls.

We talked about the perils of being surrounded by morbidity and mortality and the challenge of staying balanced and grounded in such an environment, which cannot help but give a distorted view of the world. They showed interest in my change of career and I found myself explaining the transition from nursing to reiki and massage with more clarity than ever before. They were really interested and complimented me by saying,

"You have a very peaceful air about you."

I thought that was lovely of them to say, then they called me inspiring, which was delightful to hear too. I know that other people have said it before but I am always grateful to receive such a compliment. The thing is that I often forget how far I have come and how my journey seems to others. I suspect that our conversation was striking a chord with them, particularly as one of the ladies said that she had recently read an article about the link between happiness and job satisfaction. It said that even if you are good at it, working hard to achieve and progress in a profession, is not going to provide happiness without passion for what you do. Precisely.

We had fun together, time passed quickly and we parted expecting to meet again at the evening dance.

*

Crossing the courtyard with the pretty landscaping and water feature, a gentleman I had not met before, asked if I had enjoyed my dinner. I told him that I had indeed enjoyed it and we talked about what we had eaten, then very soon we were deep in conversation about our work. He too was an energy worker living a life incorporating regular meditation. Based in Totnes, Devon his environment is quite a contrast to mine but I always maintain that our work is of value wherever it is carried out. He said that there was more need for my work in Metropolis because of the lifestyle but I believe that wherever we choose to be, the people who need us will find us and everyone benefits.

We discussed the challenge of deciding what to call ourselves for the purpose of marketing and advertising. For example, calling myself a massage therapist has its own limitations. Notwithstanding the preconceptions, it does not tell people how I do what I do, although they think they already know. I was interested to hear that he left London seven years ago to start his business in Devon and I said that I have always thought it must be fun to live in a holiday destination. We talked about rising to the challenge of consistent meditation and preserving the good feeling of well-being and inner peace that it brings. We had both experienced the ease with which these feelings can be achieved on retreats but the work then is to maintain those benefits back in the home, work and social environment. To stay grounded, to stay balanced, to stay connected, that is where the work is, that is what I feel I continue to achieve.

Carole Chandler

Our conversation flowed easily, our conversation flowed comfortably, we experienced a quick connection. Afterwards I noted that the interaction would not have taken place if I had left the ladies at the dinner table a few seconds later. I did not wait for them, I left when the impulse took me. Once again following my guidance led me to a rendezvous with a wonderful person.

*

After dinner I was preparing myself for the evening's milonga, which is the fancy name for the tango social dances. At the late breakfast earlier in the day, I had overheard a group of women at another table talking about dancing at milongas and their perceived difficulties of how to 'get more dances'. They gave reasons why some women are asked to dance and others are not. They told each other how to increase their chances of receiving invitations to dance and shared opinions on why some of them do not enjoy offers of the frequency that they thought would increase their happiness. They said a lot of things that I have heard a squillion times before and am frankly tired of it. Books have been written about it, forums devote pages to this same subject. I realise why they say it, I realise that the more they discuss it, the more real it appears but I am still tired of it. The points of view seem to stem mostly from the insecurity of leaders and followers, including a perceived level of competence and confidence.

I choose not to buy into the mindset that encourages me to worry about the probability of being asked to dance, or of how many dances I may have. I prefer to leave all of that to universal forces. Somewhere during the dress, jewellery, shoes adorning process, I made time to meditate which felt great and brought me to a place of feeling damn good about myself, other people, my life and the world in general. It also succeeded in inducing the feeling that there was only the possibility of having all the perfect dances I could ever want.

I found the hall already active with several couples walking the tango walk around the floor, to the familiar sound of the bandaneon, an instrument specific to traditional Argentine tango music. I sat, I changed my shoes, I looked around just enjoying the feeling of the space. Within a few minutes in my peripheral vision I saw a man walking towards me from the other side of the room. It was the musical analyser from the dinner table. I have no idea why but I said something I would not normally say,

"Have you forgiven me?"

He replied, "Forgiven you for what, for being a charming dinner companion? You were lovely."

Well who would have thought it? If I had been inclined to give it consideration I would have concluded that he had a completely differing opinion of me. How lovely that all was well. He asked me to dance and it was a lovely set of three dances, bless him.

Sitting down enjoying the music again, another man appeared from the opposite side of the room and treated me to another set of dances, all most enjoyable indeed.

Then another gentleman, then another gentleman, then another, I enjoyed dances with nine guys all for two to five tracks each. It was a splendid evening. They all asked me to dance, I did not ask one of them, well why would I? It would be fine to ask them if I wanted to but that is not the way I wanted it to be, nothing to do with tradition, just my personal preference. Neither did I feel the impulse to play the eye contact game, which even has a special name in the world of tango. I hear people coaching each other on the tango eye contact how-to-signal-you-want-a-dance and how-to-signal-acceptance-to-the-offer game. If I thought it would be fun I would play it but on that particularly evening, I chose to just allow myself to be myself and see what happened. I was happy with the way things went, I had fun and that was the goal after all.

Absolutely exhausted after a long day of being a tourist, meeting new people, talking to strangers, tango lessons and dancing I went to bed and left the others to it.

One more universal rendezvous happened to make me laugh before I left. I popped out to get a drink and when I returned a lady was sitting on the seat where I had originally sat and where I had left my bag, shoes and shawl. Naturally this was not an issue, what made me chuckle was that the lady sitting there was the very same Parisienne who I had sat with at dinner and with whom I had enjoyed such lively conversation. She did not even know that I had arrived yet, she did not know that I had already been dancing, she did not know where I was sitting, it was a fair sized room with lots of seats, yet she sat in the same one that I had chosen. Some might think coincidence, I think not.

*

Sunday morning once again I slept like a dream, woke up not aching too excessively but confident that this day would be a good day to take it easy. Regardless of how I might look, what I might think and what I might tell myself, I sometimes need to remember the importance of rest and recuperation because late nights and excessive dancing take their toll.

In the breakfast queue, a guy I had danced with briefly in the class the previous day turned towards me and introduced himself. I laughed when he said his name because it is the same name I call all of my gorgeous men, who collectively make up my ideal partner, in my imaginary good feeling emotional place. He said he is from Cork which is 'the real capital of Ireland'. I asked him if that is what people say in Cork and he replied,

"Oh yes, they say it because it's true."

I laughed, never having heard that before and his accent was truly delicious, I could have listened to him all day, to be sure, to be sure, to be sure.

A lady I met in my first dance class on the Friday, was next to me in the queue. We had previously exchanged names but I could not remember hers, we had nodded to each other in passing during the weekend but not spoken. While choosing breakfast, she shared her feelings about the weekend. She was having mixed emotions about the event, having a less than enjoyable time and not feeling good about herself.

I said, "Today will be fine, today will be much better."

She said, "Thank you. If you say it will be better, then I know it will be."

I asked her why she said that and she went on to tell me that when she tries to be positive, it does not work but she believed that as it was me saying it, then she had more hope. I continued,

"There you go, your day will be better, I will make it so."

I chose to end the conversation there, I felt no need to hear the specifics about why she was despondent. In my heart I wished her well and that carries far more power than to join her in her misery. I purposely made the decision not to sit with her for breakfast. As sweet as she was, her mood was too low for me, I could always catch up with her later, if I felt so inclined.

Just for the record, I bumped into her later between classes in the afternoon and she smiled saying brightly, that she felt much better and was having a far better day, just like I said she would. Apparently it did not take her long to snap out of her earlier mood and we both agreed that the improvement was preferable to spending her whole day in sadness.

*

I glanced around the dining room and spotted my delightful French ladies sitting with a couple of other people. After a "may I join you" I was warmly greeted and sat with them. Oh dear, what had I done? Had I made a mistake? They were all speaking a vitesse in French. Now that there were four of them, I wondered if they were to spend the entire time conversing in French and exclude me. I wondered if I had found myself in a similar position as the previous day at the breakfast table.

Well how silly of me to even entertain such a notion. My momentary fears were totally unfounded. Surely I realised that this day's interaction could not be so different to our friendly evening meal the day before. One of my amazing Parisiennes looked at me with her beautiful sweet smile and brought me up to speed. I had arrived when they were just talking about money and saying that the ideal life would be to travel around the world, going from one tango festival to another but wondered what they could do to finance it.

I said, "That's easy, all you do is get someone to pay you for travelling around the world going from one festival to another."

They all laughed and immediately I felt more able to see myself enjoying breakfast with them. I was simply saying something that I believe is not only an option but also a possibility and apparently they laughed because one of the group members had just said the very same thing. The other two French speakers were both from Switzerland and all four of them were truly quite delightful people. One works for a bank and our conversation was predominantly about money, people with lots of it, people who like people with lots of it and how to meet people who have lots of it.

How interesting to rendezvous with a subject like this. I would not have been that comfortable years ago, talking so freely about enjoying money. I was unaware that it was okay to admit to enjoying the freedom and security that money brings. I was unaware that abundance is a natural state of being, which is available to all of us, if we wish it and learn to allow it. Gone are the days of repeating the limiting beliefs about affluence and wealth.

So back to our breakfast conversation, we talked light heartedly about going out for a meal on a date and the man paying for the pleasure of his date's company. The Swiss lady said that she has heard of some women being independent now and wanting to pay for themselves. I mused that there must be different definitions for independence and reminded myself, each to their own. I looked at one of the French ladies, she looked at me and we both shrugged our shoulders. No words were necessary, we both knew that we agreed with each other. We burst out laughing at our joint understanding. I offered my fist, knuckles forward (a little acknowledgement of affirmation I have learned from my children), she tapped her fist against mine. Who needs words when we had communicated so perfectly.

*

Before my afternoon workshop, I found myself in the refreshment room chatting to a lady I had not seen before, who introduced herself as originally from Liverpool but living in Dublin. She had also lived in Wales and Newcastle. Well, well, well, there must be something in that. I mean that is a real collection of strong accents, how wonderful. Mind you, I guess that depends on your perspective. One of the French ladies told me earlier that I have a really strong London accent which made me laugh because only once before has anyone ever commented on my accent. I have travelled all over the world and where was the comment made? It was in Leeds! I went there to visit a friend many moons ago and we were out with some of her local friends and to my surprise they made fun of my accent. I was young and I could not see how that was even possible, as they were all Northerners. They teased me mercilessly and spent far too much of the evening rattling out comedy sketches by the two Ronnies.

Anyway, I digress. Another lady joined us, she happily told us that she is from Dublin but with shoulders drooped, head down and a groan, said depressingly in an I-hate-to-say-it kind of way, "I'm a doctor." Oh dear, I could feel her pain (no pun intended). I looked at her and said,

"That's an interesting way to say it, if you don't like being a doctor, you can stop being a doctor."

She looked at me and replied sternly, "No I can't."

I've had this conversation before and I stayed with it because it felt like it might be worth it.

"Yes you can," I replied calmly, "you don't have to be a doctor forever."

She persisted, "Yes you do have to be a doctor forever."

I can be persistent too, "No you don't."

She started to reply with another "Yes I do …" then stopped, paused, her facial expression changed and she said, "You're right, I don't have to be a doctor forever."

It was quiet, no one spoke. Then I said, "There you are, that feels better doesn't it?"

She seemed intrigued, "Why do you say that, are you are doctor?"

The attention was then on me, as they waited for a response. I told them that I am not but have worked with many and have had this conversation before. I have met others who did not want to be doctors any more either.

I told them about a conversation I had with a neonatal registrar, who I had the pleasure of working with many years ago. Once again she was run ragged and feeling the exhaustion. She had previously joked about leaving the profession and working for a well-known department store. When I asked her what she would ideally like to spend her life doing if she had the courage to leave, she knew her answer immediately. Her passion was hats, she liked designing hats, she wanted to be a milliner.

The tango doctor perked up and said, "Oh it's funny you should say that because I'm learning to be a milliner, I love making hats." Bingo. So, there was her discomfort. I shared my thoughts with her. Making hats is creative, she enjoys being creative and she is in a job where she does not get to use her creativity, so she is being pulled in different directions. She looked at me somewhat blankly, unintentionally I am sure, then seemed to snap out of it.

"Well, I've gone private, it's not full time anymore and it pays the bills." As if happy with her justification, she disappeared out of the room. Her exit was quite dramatic. If it were a pantomime, I might have expected an accompanying puff of smoke.

Bless her, I never saw her again. I really have no attachment either way to the outcome of the conversation. It is of no consequence to me whether she stayed as a doctor or became an international milliner much requested by the rich and famous. I just want her to be happy.

*

After our doctor disappeared, a lady, who had been present and silent during the conversation, told me that she makes hats. Really? Even I wondered about the possibility of coincidence when she said that. Nah, I am only kidding, I never wonder about coincidence, I know that *'like attracts like'*. For the past three years she had been a full time milliner and selling her creations successfully in her local vintage clothing shop, where she had a good arrangement with the owner.

Sounded like all was working out well for her, which was great and we talked about the transition when changing from a career providing regular fixed income, to one where you enjoy the passion of your creativity but sometimes the financial rewards take time to catch up. She was great, I enjoyed chatting to her and it was lovely to hear that good things were happening for her.

I enjoyed my last class of the weekend, indeed my last class of the festival. They were fun and they were technical, it was interesting to experience the diversity within the groups, from some guys who had it sussed immediately to others who seemed to struggle. In this class the instructor spent some extra one to one time with one of my partners, afterwards we tried again and he thanked me for my patience. Then he hit me with a bombshell. He said that his first tango lesson was during the festival that very same weekend.

Well with a hint of an accent as he spoke, I was not totally sure that I had heard him correctly. Perhaps he meant to say something else. Perhaps he had intended to use different words to convey a different meaning. Perhaps I had misunderstood. It would not have been the first time during the fun weekend, as there had been a lot of repeated dialogue, while dancers from all over Europe conversed with each other. Never mind England and Ireland, I met people from France, Germany, Holland, Belgium, Italy, Norway, Sweden, Austria and most of them with exceptional English but understandably with the occasional misuse of a word here and there.

I thought it would be prudent to clarify, so I asked,

"Your first tango lesson?"

"Yes."

"This weekend?"

"Yes."

"Your first tango lesson, ever?"

"Yes."

Well it was hardly any wonder he found the class challenging. We were working on a technical move and in Argentine tango, many people spend at least the first couple of years, concentrating on walking forwards and backwards, before tackling the tricky stuff. Hey, you do not have to take my word for it, feel free to ask any tango fan. This man must have been some kind of genius to do as well as he did, I congratulated him, encouraged him to stay with it, he thanked me again and we moved on.

By way of contrast, the next guy I partnered had no such mountain to climb, he nailed the move. He was so comfortable with the new skill that he led it in both directions, which is not something that many leaders can boast and is always impressive.

The lesson came to an end and the music changed. I found myself with a guy who was happy to forget the subject of the class and just dance for the pleasure of it. What a pleasure it was too. He took me in his arms and within seconds I knew, I just knew that I was in heaven. His expertise captivated me. I was whisked off to a place where few leaders have transported me. He led, I followed, we danced. It could have been a minute, an hour, a day, a week, a year, I had no cares. I closed my eyes. I believe it is fair to say that it is a rare follower who would choose to close her eyes when dancing with someone for the first time. Even when in the arms of a familiar leader it is an indication of feeling safe, secure and at one with all that is wonderful. So, there I was, I closed my eyes and drifted into bliss.

Experiences like that, are the reason why I tango.

*

Earlier during the class I had enjoyed a brief chat with a lovely gentleman who captured my attention. Looking good, sounding charming and dancing pretty damn confidently, he had qualities I liked. I was interested.

At the end of the lesson I looked for him, sat next to him and engaged him in conversation, I liked him, really liked him, he was easy on the eye, easy to talk to and his charm was working on me whether he intended it or not. Here was the first person I had met on this holiday, who made me think, mmm... I would like to see more of you. Well that is all well and good but is pointless unless it is mutual. Another class was about to begin and we were not taking part, so we left the room. He wandered off, there were other people to chat to, so I sat in the practice room, changed my shoes thinking more and more that I would fancy the opportunity to talk to him more and get to know him better.

It was early evening and I toyed with the idea of asking him if he had plans for dinner just to see if that prompted him. As soon as the thought crossed my mind, I dismissed it as not only out of character but not the story I want to tell. So I did the best thing I know, I handed it over to the Universe.

Moments later he came in and made a general announcement in the room,

"Does anyone want to go for a bite to eat?"

The first thing I did was thank the Universe because I knew he had been sent in for me, then I joined a few other people in saying yes to the wonderful idea. I have no doubts of my own but this is yet another demonstration of how the Universe takes care of requests sometimes as soon as we ask. I wanted to spend more time with him and a couple of hours eating out with him and a wonderful bunch of people would be just the ticket.

*

Our dinner crew gathered at reception with coats, bags and brollies ready to face the weather. As I had enjoyed it so much on the day of my arrival, I suggested the Thai restaurant about a fifteen minute walk away. Did I mind walking in the rain? Was I bothered about getting wet? I decided that it did not matter as my clothes would dry by the morning. We were four guys and two gals, one I had met briefly the day before but did not remember his name and a couple I had met for the first time that day. It was going to be fun, I could feel it.

It was raining heavily and I was ready to walk, then as luck would have it one of the guys said that as I knew the way, I could go in his car to give directions. Car, what did he mean car?

"Don't forget I'm a local, so I have a car."

Well I knew he was Irish but I had not registered that he was local, so it was great that he had transport. It had not occurred to me because I was in vacation mode and thought they were too. Well when I saw the car, I burst out laughing but could not explain why, well, not to them anyway. I laughed because it was a Lexus and I get very excited whenever I see a Lexus, I have no explanation for it just that the Lexus is my favourite car and I was happy to see it be part of my experience on our trip to dinner. I thanked the Universe again. One day I may tell the story of the Lexus sports driver I had a fun interaction with in a supermarket car park.

Oh what the heck, I'll tell it now. So I had been driving around south London one afternoon, enjoying a bit of Lexus spotting and had already seen seven when I pulled into a supermarket car park. I had never been to this store before and was in the south west London area of Fulham to check out a new development of luxury apartments that appealed to me. As I locked my car doors, a tan coloured Lexus sports with the top down, pulled up in front of me. The driver was deep in conversation on his phone. I strolled over to the windscreen and made an obvious show of looking around in appreciation, nodding and smiling and making a quiet fuss of his lovely vehicle. He stopped talking, looked at me and smiled, I continued to enjoy his car, I was in no hurry, someone was waiting for him on the phone, I was not about to interrupt.

He abruptly ended his phone conversation and told them that he had to go. Well what a treat, he was a fine figure of a man and did not fit the stereotype of men who drive sports cars and compensating and so on. He was cute, or buff, or whatever word we are using now to describe men who turn heads. However, it was the car that had my attention, not him. I was genuinely interested in the car, so we talked about how much fun it is to drive, the fuel consumption, his personally chosen additional specifications, he was happy to give information and I was happy to listen. That was it. End of interaction.

So where was I before that little tale? Ah yes, I was happy to be the navigator in the front of a Lexus. At dinner the guys who were Dubliners talked about dodgy drinking venues and their association with less reputable members of the community (not the guys but the venues). They mentioned places that they were unwilling to go. I told them that I had been enjoying my adventures and happily wandering into places new to me. I did not know the districts like they did, so I asked them how I could be sure that I would not find myself in one of these areas or drinking holes by accident. Well they assured me that these places were so obvious, I would not even consider going in. Well that was good to know.

150

On the way in the car I talked about how much I was enjoying my holiday and mentioned the fun with the nun at the bus stop episode. They laughed so hard I wondered why they seemed to find it funnier than I did. One of the said,

"I wonder if she understood the irony of it."

As we had split our group between two cars the others had not heard my tale, so at the restaurant, the guys I had travelled with insisted,

"Tell the others your joke about the nun."

Well, I assured them all that it was not a joke, it was real and it actually happened to me. I began and after a few words the same guy stopped me again and said,

"No, start again, tell it like a joke."

Well I know my limitations and joke telling is not my forté but I decided to oblige and said,

"A funny thing happened to me while I was waiting for the bus..."

Seriously now, why were they putting me under pressure, I am not an Irish stand-up comedian. Perhaps in the company of Dara or Ed one might say 'go on tell it like a joke' but not poor little me. I struggled to tell the story at all because those that had heard it in the car and clearly enjoyed it, kept interrupting me and prompting me, "tell them about the ..." and "don't forget the bit about ..." I am delighted that they were so tickled.

*

The meal was delicious, the company wonderful and it was time well spent. Someone mentioned the time and some of them wanted to return for the evening's dancing. I tried not to be unhappy but I was a teeny bit sad at the thought of leaving because I was having such a great time. Well we still had dessert and coffees to be served, as the remainder of our reasonably priced set meal, so we clearly were not going to be rushing off that quickly. The lady said,

"Sorry Carole, I know you like to take things slowly." Hey, how did she know that? Apparently I had mentioned it earlier in the day, during our conversation about life, the Universe and all manner of things. I had said something in passing about realising some time ago that a great de-stressor in life is to take things much slower. It works for me.

Ah yes I remember how it came about. I was in the refreshment room after a class, I helped myself to a cup of tea and a snack and sat to enjoy. A lady asked how my feet were coping with all of the dancing and I told her that they were coping surprisingly well, considering. She asked if I rub them to make them feel better and I confessed that I am often playing with my feet and we all agreed that it helps. Someone else joined in, saying that she never thinks of it and I told her that massaging my feet really makes a difference to how they feel in the morning. We were talking about our feet but I was idly wondering to myself, how we had been a group since Friday and it was now Sunday afternoon and I could not recall seeing any of these three women before. Oh well, back to the feet.

Carole Chandler

I kicked off my shoes and showed them how I massage the sole of one foot, with the heel of the other. I told them that it is a way of applying pressure, without using your thumbs and fingers, which can become pretty sore much quicker, without achieving the same pressure anyway. It was fun to watch them all have a go, as I held my mini workshop. How funny. I disappeared for a few minutes and when I returned one lady remained. As I sat again, she said that she liked trying to massage her feet herself and that I was right they felt better. Her shoes were off and she rubbed her heel quickly along the sole of her foot. Oh dear, there are many ways to skin a cat I thought.

"Well done, but it can be uncomfortable with your receiving foot on the floor, it's a bit hard for you. It's easier on a bed or something softer. Try putting your foot on the chair."

She moved furniture and tried again. She still rubbed quickly and although the way she did it was absolutely fine, I felt inspired to offer a suggestion.

"Move slower, massage your foot slower with your heel, nice and slow, caress your foot with firm but gentle pressure. Love your foot."

Her expression changed, it softened and with a whimsical look she said,

"Ooh, you're good Carole." Without thinking about it and without doubt I said,

"I know."

That was when I went on to say some stuff about doing things slower, much slower. Life is good, life is better when I take my time. I thought quietly to myself, that my challenge, my quest now is to find people to enjoy my life slowly with me.

Anyway, back to the restaurant. The Irish lads talked about how much their country has changed during the last ten years. I learned how it was a big deal when England played rugby against Ireland at the Crowe Park ground which is traditionally home to Gaelic football. We were told about northern and southern Ireland differences and how relationships have improved. There was some banter about potato famines and poverty but I do not know much about that. Someone mentioned the diversity of our group and that us sitting and enjoying an evening together was evidence of how far we have all come. We were from several countries and backgrounds so it was evidence indeed.

At some point during our lively conversations one of the chaps said to me,

"You've travelled here on your own." Well I was feeling relaxed, almost forgetting that I hardly knew any of them, so I responded truthfully,

"Yes, I'm on my own but I'm not alone."

Oh dear, maybe I should not have said that, perhaps these lovely people were not ready to hear that. I usually wait until I know people at least a little better before I drop the, I'm-on-my-own-but-I'm-not-alone bombshell.

"What do you mean?" I tried to say that it did not matter but he insisted,

"Well, it's too late you've said it now, what do you mean, on your own but not alone?"

Quick, I had to be quick, I had to think quickly, the whole table was waiting for my response. I asked for guidance, for how to proceed. My answer came immediately in the form of our waitress arriving with a tray of delicious ice cream desserts, which distracted everyone sufficiently, so I was off the hook. Phew, that was close. There is a time and a place and I do not think it was either there or then.

The others were keen to dance, I was keen to rest, so we left. He who originally had my attention, still had my attention. During our meal, there was nothing about him that lessened my interest. I liked him and would

Carole Chandler

have been happy to spend more time with him. However, like I said before, there is no point unless it is mutual. The universe lines us up but does not interfere with free will. He did not ask. We said our fond goodbyes, with hugs and expectations to see each other on the tango circuit and we parted. Pity, but not so much.

Moving on…

*

Up bright and early Monday morning. So relieved that I did not go dancing Sunday night, it would have been simply too much. Gone are the days when I would dance on a weekender from Friday night to Monday morning, forgetting to eat or sleep. I have never been a night person anyway, which leaves me at a slight disadvantage with dancing as my hobby. Tea dances yes, start and finish in daylight, bed at a reasonable hour, up with the lark as preferred, consequently with far less suffering and far less muscle aching.

I walked into the dining room for breakfast and was surprised to see quite so many of the tango crew. Picking up my tray I helped myself to a bowl of porridge with walnuts and raisins, the same breakfast I had enjoyed every day during my stay at this illustrious establishment. A woman put her tray beside mine and smiled saying,

"I saw you the day I arrived, we checked in at the same time."

Well that was sweet of her to remember me, though I did not remember seeing her either then or any other time during the weekender. I am convinced that I would have remembered her because what I definitely had not noticed before, was her fabulous hair. Wow, her hair was beautiful. All thick and long and straight with a glorious selection of colours from dark brown to silver with sections of gold, bronze, copper and amber, giving a profusion of beauty in her silky strands. Her beautiful hair framed her equally beautiful face and was loosely held by a beautiful claw clip half way down her back, draping her shoulders like a silk scarf.

I was so surprised that I had not noticed her hair before because it was certainly unmissable right there at the Monday morning breakfast counter. I could hardly take my eyes off it. I have been distracted by hair before, I have been known to compliment women on buses and walking along the road and luckily they have always been happy to hear it.

I could not contain myself, I had to tell her that her hair was gorgeous. She began to reply, "Oh really, its …"

She gave one of those responses that women often give when they do not appreciate their own inherent beauty and gifts. I was not really listening. I have heard it all before and had no intention of joining her in any hair negativity, especially as I was far too busy admiring it. Why should I contain myself? It feels good to admire and appreciate. It feels even better when the receiver is even close to knowing the same. However, it is not necessary and does not stop me inwardly expressing, although, depending on the person I many choose not to outwardly express.

So I felt inspired to continue,

"Yes, your hair is really lovely, it's beautifully thick and long and look at the colours, they're fabulous."

She stopped her mild protesting, seemed to listen and thanked me. I asked her if she ever plaits it, to which she said,

"Yes, sometimes I do one on each side." Putting my hand on the top of her head, I asked whether she ever does a French plait on the back.

"Oh yes, I like it like that, my mother used to do it but I don't know how to do it myself." Well I could not think of anything I would rather do, so I offered to plait it for her. When she realised that I was serious, I was not joking, I really wanted to plait her hair purely for the fun of doing it, she seemed delighted and said excitedly,

"What, now?"

Okay, let's not get carried away, after breakfast would be fine. She thanked me for the offer, I thanked her for accepting, she thanked me again and we could have been there a long time, playing thank you tennis but I nipped it in the bud.

*

All set and ready to eat, I sat with the lovely, handsome, amusing, charming, friendly Swiss gent I had met at breakfast the previous day. He said that the French ladies were still in bed "getting their beauty sleep", I cheekily told him that I did not need any more as I was beautiful enough to cope with my day. Bless him for agreeing me.

This reminded me of a visit I made to an organic beauty product emporium in London, which was promoting a beauty serum at substantial prices with the promise of beauty in a jar. All that was required was application before bed time, with noticeable results in the morning. I pointed out that the good night's sleep is largely responsible for the difference, with or without the promised elixir.

Anyway, back to breakfast. The lady with the fab hair sat beside me, well of course she did. After all I had made a hair connection with her so why would she not choose to sit next to me? I am not being funny but I almost forgot she was there, as she was very quiet and I mostly engaged with a few other quite strong characters at the table.

For example a chap sat on the other side of me with a full plate of fried, well, everything. He was clearly hungry and not taking himself too seriously because when he finished he left the table and returned with his plate as loaded as before, with another selection of fried everything. I think they call it A Full English, well no kidding, it would have filled many an English. His second plate of egg, bacon, sausage, tomatoes, mushrooms, black pudding, potato things and toast disappeared just like the first. Woah, how was he doing that? Was he a large man? No not at all. He was small, thin, I do not want to say he was tiny but he was tiny. I failed to see how a frame so small could consume quantities of food so large. If he were even marginally overweight, I would have thought nothing of his food choice and ignored the two plates of fried everything. Certainly if he was large and if I had paid any attention to him, I would have had the common decency to keep my thoughts to myself. Everyone on the table had noticed and I felt the question had to be asked,

"Where is all that food going?" He laughed and said,

"I'm lucky I have always been able to eat a lot of food."

Somehow that did not answer my question, I was still gobsmacked. I looked on the floor around his seat. Perhaps he was not eating it at all, perhaps he was feeding it to a previously unnoticed, well behaved pet under the table. He laughed, we all laughed.

As if that was not enough, he left the table again and returned with a third helping. Admittedly there was less than the previous two but another full meal all the same. Now come on, it is not my nature to comment on how or what people eat. I understood a long time ago the connection between our emotional well-being and physical apparatus. I understand how food is used to fuel our body and our mind. Food can be a sensitive issue for many people, a personal issue indeed, a reflection of self-acceptance.

I said, "Look, if you're doing this for amusement, we are officially amused, you don't have to eat it, I was impressed with the other two plates, so please don't feel that you have to eat this one." He was fine, he enjoyed his food and took no notice of what I said and rightly so.

*

One of the guys asked, "Did you have a good time last night?"

When I said that I did and thanks for asking, he looked at me and waited. Then I realised that he was asking if I had enjoyed the evening dance. I admitted that I did not go and he said,

"I thought I hadn't seen you." Ooh, how sneaky, the way he asked me caught me out and I would have probably responded differently, had I realised but never mind it did not matter. It was so sweet of him to notice my absence though. Another guy joined us and he also asked why I was not dancing the night before. I thanked him too for asking and told them that I really had danced enough the whole weekend, I had no intention of pushing myself too far and another evening would have been too much. One of my stock phrases for me and people I meet is 'know when to stop'.

By now another chap had arrived and we were still talking about why I had chosen not to include the Sunday night dance in my weekend of activities. It was really very sweet of them all to notice that I was not there, it was even sweeter of them to bother asking and yes it would have been lovely to dance with them all but I explained that I had used a lot of my energy not only dancing but zipping in and out of the city being a tourist. For some reason I decided to add,

"Besides, I'm writing a book and I spent some time in the evening concentrating on that."

There, I had said it out loud to strangers. I had actually announced that I was writing a book. I had only ever mentioned that I was considering it to one other person and here I was finding the inspiration to go public.

"What is your book about?" This enquiry came from my lovely, handsome, amusing, charming, friendly Swiss gentleman, "is it a thriller, crime, fantasy?"

Ooh, he was asking a question about my book, this was a conversation never had before. I was unprepared. I decided to follow my gut.

"It's none of those, it is about my travels." That felt okay, it seemed like the right thing to say at the time.

"What are you writing about your travels, is it like a guide or your experiences?" Ooh er, that was a great question, I could see where he was coming from.

"It's about my experiences." That felt okay, it seemed like the right thing to say at the time.

"So for your experiences, are you gathering material or is it about funny things that happen." Ooh er, another great question, he was interested, it was time to open up.

"It's really about my experiences, things that happen to me and the people I meet. I always meet people wherever I go and funny things do happen, yes. I'm keeping it light."

"Sounds good, I'm sure your book will be good." Oh how supportive of him to make a positive comment. I thanked him and congratulated myself on my introduction to the world of the press release.

Another chap interjected, "Yes but you're not actually writing it are you, you don't physically write do you?" I looked at him not quite understanding. I must have looked confused because he added,

"Well, you're not physically writing are you, it's typed on a computer." I proceeded to enlighten him,

"Yes I am writing, physically writing with pen and paper, I have a note book and I'm writing it in there." Then he was his turn to look confused.

"Why, why would you do that? I couldn't do that, I think I might actually have forgotten how to write and anyway my hand writing is terrible." I told him that I like writing and my penmanship is not so bad. I had my note book with me and took it out of my bag to show them the dozen or so pages I had penned the night before. I proudly felt and sensed their amazement. Flicking through the pages they seemed to like my handwriting and I quite understand that, as I like my handwriting too. I flicked through the leaves of my book revealing page after page of words, sentences and paragraphs which just flowed through me with seemingly little effort the previous night after my delicious meal, washed down with strong Jasmine tea in the company of delightful people. I have no doubt that the joyous dining experience helped to increase my creativity.

"Wow, did you write all that?"

"It is so neat."

"Did you actually write all those pages?"

"Your writing is lovely."

Well, after these lovely interested questions and comments, it seemed that going public with my book might be fun after all. My lovely, handsome, amusing, charming, friendly, Swiss gent said,

"You have beautiful writing to reflect your beautiful personality."

There, you see what I mean about charming? That was such a lovely thing for him to say and for me to hear, I said,

"That is so sweet of you, thank you, feel free to say that as many times as you like."

Then I thought about it and realised something which I shared with them. Writing by hand is a different process to typing. If I typed my thoughts, I would be constantly editing because that is the tendency when using a computer. That rarely happens when I write by hand, there is a flow, a consistency and an ease with which the words just emerge from me, as I write them directly on the page. Also I find that I feel more freedom, more conversational, more natural, more in the moment. I have noticed that when I type, I tend to use short sharp phrases and sentences. I suppose this largely accounts for why email is not my chosen form of communication. It is not how I like to express myself, not really me.

Someone asked, "What do you do when you've written it?"

I told them, that then I type it on the computer, I type what I've written without needing to change it much. Apart from tweaking it here and there, I pretty much type it as it is. I went on to compare it to the difference between a hand written letter and an email received from the same person. They feel quite different. I have been known to write letters to friends abroad and post them rather than send an email. So what if it takes longer? I love the fun of it. I love the enjoyment and pleasure of giving and receiving.

The self-confessed terrible handwriting breakfast buddy said,

"Yes, but typing is so much quicker, I type really quickly now." I explained that I am not in a hurry, it does not need to be quick, time is not an issue. Seriously folks what is this obsession with speed? Never mind, the Swiss chap is a banker and he made us all laugh when he said that the only writing he does is when signing cheques. See what I mean about him being amusing?

*

That was enough talking about my book so we returned to the universal subject of dancing, our joint love of tango and other dances. One of the guys at the table was a chap I have met in the jive world. I did not know his name but we remembered dancing together, so it was fun combining the two in our conversation. Then out of the blue he passed me a piece of paper. Yay, it was an invitation, ooh how absolutely wonderful, I love invitations. It was to a party. Not just any party but his party. I did not know it but he hosts a party in his home every year and he assured me that there would be other people who I knew.

To be honest that had not even crossed my mind as a factor for consideration, I loved the idea of a party starting in the afternoon, through the evening into the night, with music for jive and tango, so I had already made the decision to go. Of course it would be nice to know people but was certainly not a necessity, as I would always find people to dance with and people to chat to. He has a temporary floor laid in the garden for fine weather and moves furniture out of the rooms to create space for dancing inside, if the weather does not hold up. He said that he even stores his bed elsewhere to make room for food and drink. I was pretty impressed by that and imagined that with so much effort going into preparations and with the promise of additional food and fun, it already had the ingredients for an enjoyable time.

Carole Chandler

We all carried on chatting about the weekend generally and I said a few things about my adventures as a tourist, on and off buses, meeting people and visiting places. I began telling my breakfast buddies about the beauty and splendour of Trinity College, when one of the guys said that he was well acquainted with the architecture because he studied mathematics and computer science at Trinity College Cambridge. Oh really, how cool is that? There was nothing I could tell him about the majesty of the place, he already knew.

The table banter about dancing, travelling, more dancing and more travelling had to come to an end at some point. As much fun as it was, it obviously could not go on forever. With breakfast finished it was time to make moves but not before the promised hair plaiting gift experience. I turned to my lady with the beautiful hair and was delighted to see that not only was she ready but excited by the prospect.

Producing a brush from her bag she began to brush her hair herself but I managed to persuade her to let me brush it for her instead. I am always happy to include brushing as part of the experience because I know how lovely it is to feel someone else play with your hair. She asked me if I am a hairdresser,

"Oh goodness me no, I just like plaiting hair so thank you for letting me play with yours."

"Well thank you for plaiting it for me," she replied. I nearly said thank you again but restrained myself as we were in serious danger of embarking on another round of thank you tennis, so once again I nipped it in the bud.

I brushed her gorgeous hair and I took my time doing it. There was no reason to rush, so I did not hurry. She sat quietly, while I divided the hair into sections at the top and gradually created a perfect design of triple woven beauty down the back of her head. I am not saying that she purred but I could feel her relax increasingly and for me it was rather like stroking a cat. At the end, I am still not saying she purred but she made a rather pleasing noise of contentment and satisfaction. That was all the thanks I could possibly have needed, if in fact thanks were required. Really, I mean it, her agreeing to allow me the pleasure of plaiting her hair was thanks enough.

Anyway, she looked at me with a soft, dreamy, faraway look in her eyes and said,

"Ooh that was really lovely, it felt so nice, like it was a massage."

I thanked her and I was glad that she liked it." She continued,

"Your hands are sooo … I could really feel your hands, they are sooo … soothing, it was so relaxing, I feel really relaxed."

She became really quite emotional and as she stroked the back of her head, she said that she felt like a film star. I felt happy that she was happy. When she told me that her mother used to plait her hair that way, I understood. We shared a moment. She held my hand and squeezed it.

I let her know that head massages are included in my field of work she said,

"Oh it's a pity we have only just met, I wish we had talked before." So far, she had felt her hair but not seen it, so I gave her a little mirror from my bag and off she went to find a large mirror, so she could view the back of her head. Well she was joyous before she left but when she returned, her joy had increased,

"I look like a mermaid", she said excitedly. Well it only felt natural for me to say,

"You can be a mermaid, you can be anything you like." She looked at me, paused and said,

Carole Chandler

"Yes I can, I can be anything I like, thank you."

The experience was over for me and I was ready to be on my way. She really was the sweetest lady and before she let me go, she handed her camera to someone else at the table and we posed for a picture together. I was flattered that she asked and then it was my turn to feel like a celebrity, it was fun, I was having fun. She was really happy with the result and when she showed me the photo, I had to take a moment myself. I had to take a moment because I looked and looked again. Was that really me? I hardly recognised myself in the picture. I looked … really … happy. I knew that I was happy but I did not realise that I looked so, well, gorgeous. She was delighted to have photographic memory of our meeting, I had not thought of doing that and I like that she was so inspired to think of it. She asked about my work, so I happily told her that relaxing people is my thing. That is what I do. I enjoy giving reiki treatments, lots of head massages, hand massages and face massages either separately or incorporated within body massages. Again she expressed disappointment that we had not met properly before because she would have liked to try one.

I laughed and expressed my surprise that I had not noticed her hair before and asked to plait it before. I told her of the time when I walked into a workshop in London and on greeting the assembled participants, I immediately announced to a woman with beautiful hair, that I would like to plait it later. During our lunch break my wish was granted. She allowed me to plait hers and so did two other ladies who formed an orderly queue. I loved it.

After the photograph it was really time to be making tracks. She promised to email the picture to me, we shared a lovely, long, wonderful, warm hug when she told me that I am a special lady. Ah, how nice.

*

One of the guys had earlier said that he might travel into the city with me, so all ready with my coat and bag I found him talking to some dancers at another table. When I told him that I was ready to leave, no one was more surprised than I, to see my lovely, handsome, amusing, charming, friendly Swiss gentleman approach me and say,

"I don't want you to say goodbye and go before having a hug from you."

I was flattered. I really was very flattered indeed. It was an honour to be asked.

When the long warm hug with him was over, imagine my surprise to find the two lovely French ladies had arrived for breakfast and were waiting for a hug too. Well get me, I had a queue. One of them complimented me, saying that I know how to hug and I thanked her in agreement. She also thanked me for the nice things I had said about her French accent. She had been less confident about speaking up because she did not feel that her English was good. However, she felt better after I had said how good her English really is and how beautiful her accent is to hear. Well it was easy for me to say that because I felt it and speak as I find.

Anyway, I took my time, never one to hurry a hug, Not bad coming from someone who is, in terms, a fairly recent member of the hugging society. By the way if one of those does not exist then perhaps it should. I know how nurturing and nourishing a hug can be, even for a short time but especially when we are warm, unhurried and totally present.

Hugging used to be unfamiliar to me, I had to learn. I remember attending my first meditation weekend workshop, which was run by a couple in a huge rambling house in Oxford. I was already a little apprehensive about not knowing what to expect but positively knew that something needed to be done about me, how I felt about me, how I felt about my life and how I perceived the world around me.

The husband greeted me at the door with an almighty, enveloping hug of such duration and pressure that it freaked me out. Ouch! Why was he holding me so close? Why was he squeezing so tight? I had no idea what he was doing or why he was doing it but I wanted it to stop. To this day I do not know what prevented me from turning and running away immediately because that is what I wanted to do. I can laugh about it now and in retrospect it reminds me of the scene in Fawlty Towers, where Basil displays affection towards Sybil, "What are you doing Basil? ... Well don't"

Surely it is testament to the fact that I knew I had serious work to do, which made me endure the gross discomfort of a hug, in order to learn what might be done, to enable my personal growth. I am proud of myself for sticking with it.

As for the group hug, the first time I witnessed one of those I was quite distressed by the sight. They may as well have been involved in some kind of initiation, peculiar to an illegal underground cult, for all the sense it made to me at the time. I was on my first self-improvement-find-yourself residential weekend course, the first of many I might add. It is safe to say that the group hug was voluntary and I kept well clear, I wanted no part of it. I felt so confused. For goodness sake, what on earth was going on? Why oh why were they doing that? I had serious concerns for the people in the middle, surely they needed to be helped, to be rescued. I was convinced that they were not there through choice.

Now, years later it would seem that I am a hug proficient. People who hardly know me ask for hugs. I was never asked before. Well I have made up for it now and am ever ready as the hugger and the huggee. With several meditation, self-improvement weekends added to my portfolio, the mere mention of a group hug started to find me in the middle, willing to soak it all up, agreeing to share in any amount of warmth being offered and love being spread.

So after that brief account of my hugging history, let us return to the breakfast departure. With hugs requested and hugs granted, real hugs with bags put down and arms fully extended to signal willing receptivity. Not a one second shoulder variety of hug but a body, it's-been-really-wonderful-to-meet-you-and-I-will-fondly-remember-our-interaction-for-a-long-time-and-I-wish-for-you everything-that-you-would-wish-for-yourself kind of hug. Yes, I think that just about sums it up.

*

So it begs the question, was it a big deal to be asked for a hug? Well not now, it is not a big deal now I suppose but over the years in conjunction with my increasing awareness, I came to learn of the power that a hug brings. It has been a big deal in the past but is less so now.

How about the hair plaiting episode, was it a big deal to plait her hair? Not really but there is an associated element of trust and during a plaiting session, I have experienced some emotional outpourings from others, especially regarding their maternal relationships, so I know that good comes of it.

Time has passed and I have done a lot of work on myself, a lot of work indeed. I have ironed out a few things, well a lot of things really, I have banished demons and befriended others. Limiting beliefs have been eliminated and replaced by positive, joy creating, life enhancing beliefs. The work has afforded me the opportunity to do one overriding very important thing, which has made the most difference.

I am finally allowing myself to be me.

*

I am not really sure how it came about but somehow I had agreed to let one of the chaps from our lively breakfast table crowd accompany me to the city. I was happy for the company but not dependent upon it, I had clear intentions for my last day as a tourist in Dublin's fair city and I sincerely hoped, that I was not going to have to let him know that my plans were not subject to negotiation. I think that says more about my past experiences, than about him.

Anyway, he had made plans to meet a couple of the girls for lunch and had a plane to catch later, so I had no idea how his schedule was going to neatly flow alongside mine but I reminded myself that none of that was my concern. All I had to do was focus on my intention, be aware of my feelings and all would be well.

I was keen to use my new one day rambler ticket on my last day and visit places that I had passed on buses. Our first bus arrived within a minute and we had a swift journey to the city. Waiting for the second bus my tourist buddy asked if we really needed to wait for the bus and said that we could just as easily walk. He was right we could but I wanted to catch the bus, so we did. One of the many things which I have learned is that no one has to do anything, we all get to choose. I reminded myself of the importance of allowing myself to be me and that my new companion was at liberty to stay or leave at any moment if he wished.

The question of whether to bus or walk, may on the surface seem a minor issue. In essence it is, however it is indicative of changed patterns of behaviour. In the past, I have altered my plans to fit in with others. I have put their preferences before my own, in order to please. I have been guilty of ignoring my own needs to put others first. I have learned not to do that anymore. I have learned that if my response to a suggestion is 'hell yes' then do it, so that is my guide. I only agree if I want to, even if a part of me is not keen, for whatever reason, then my answer is simply no and justification is not required. In short, I remember to follow my inner guidance. Some may call it my feelings, my gut, my instincts or my intuition, they are all different ways of expressing the same thing I suppose. Everything flows when we do this, well everything flows when I do, as I said before, I do not speak for others any more.

*

First stop was St Stephen's Green. I had passed it several times during the previous few days and I just felt the urge to check it out. A couple of bus stops later we were there and it was worth the trip. The park is beautiful. I loved the landscaping, the design and the symmetry of the beautifully planted flower beds near the pond. The central bed was full of some large petalled, yellow creations which looked like a cross between tulips and lilies. My tourist buddy said that they looked like individual people and he was right.

On the pond I spotted a swan. It was a lone swan, I looked for its companion but I did not see another. It was chilling at the far side of the pond looking majestic, well it is hard for a swan not to look royal. I gave my camera to my buddy and asked him to take a picture of me, with the swan in the background. At the same moment that I asked him, the swan came over to our side of the water, stopping beside me in the perfect position for the photograph. No he did not leave the water, he knew that was not necessary, he posed and I posed. I turned and thanked him, then the swan proceeded to elegantly and gracefully glide away. How cool was that? Very obliging I thought too.

Walking away to enjoy another area of these beautiful gardens I told my buddy, that I have often fancied that I was a swan in a previous life. He said,

"Well swans are graceful and elegant and you are graceful and elegant."

Woah, that was lovely to hear. Just between you and me, I pretended that I had not heard him, so that he would have to say it again, as it felt so good.

It was interesting for me to receive a response like that because back in the days when I attracted the company of a very different kind of personality, back in the days when I felt less sure of myself, back in the days when I did not possess the awareness that I find so familiar now, back in the days when I was ignorant of my power, back in the days when I searched for approval outside of myself, way back then, I had been subjected to very different responses to the same statement. Thank goodness those days are behind me. Now I know that I have my own approval. I had come a long way and there I was in a park, in another country, with a chap I recently met, who was seeing me the way I wish to be seen and responding in the way I liked.

*

Leaving the park for the next stage of my planned day to bus across town to the zoo, I popped into the shopping centre to avail myself of the facilities and was amused to see a chap sat outside taking money and giving change for the loos. It was fun to see him, as I am so used to automated barriers for entry to public conveniences at home. It was lovely to see a human interacting with people going by and he even looked happy to be there too.

On my way out, I met a lady in the lift, with her baby all snuggled up in the buggy. He seemed content under a roof of clear plastic in preparation for the rain outside. I chatted to the baby who smiled and chuckled at me, which was nice. I was glad to see that my English accent did not confuse him, then again I strongly suspect that he was not responding to what I said but to how I said it. His mother had a lovely, soft Irish accent and seemed happy to tell me, as we descended two floors in the lift, that her cute baby had just been fed and changed, that she expected him to fall asleep in the buggy, that walking would send him off to sleep, giving her more time to enjoy her shopping. Well, that was all fairly familiar. I have had that same conversation with many a young mother in England, so no difference between London and Dublin then.

As I met up with my buddy again he said, "I'd like to come to the zoo with you but there is something I'd like to do first, I'd like to sit somewhere for a coffee."

My guidance was clear, his idea sounded okay, I was comfortable with that so, I told him I was happy to sit somewhere first too. If my instinct was to say no for any reason that would have been fine as well.

Browsing a lovely city centre shopping street we spotted a café that looked nice enough from the outside. Well that was an understatement. We were led across the ground floor to the other side of the building that seemed to go on forever. Alright, alright, I exaggerate but you get the picture. The décor was not just beautiful but so beautiful it took my breath away. The windows of glorious stained glass imagery, depicted people and garlands around pillars, which reminded me of some of the beautiful pieces I had viewed in the gallery, a couple of days earlier. There were huge oil paintings to decorate the large wall spaces too. The large, glowing chandeliers hanging from the high ceilings were a joy to behold.

I was seated on a red, velvet, embroidered, padded seat, the beautiful wooden tables dotted about gave the place a regal atmosphere. My peppermint tea was like any other but my almond croissant was one of the most delicious I have ever tasted. It was warm, (which in my view always enhances the whole almond croissant experience) with almond paste in the middle, (which in my view always enhances the whole almond croissant experience) mmm ... yummy. If anyone reading this enjoys almond croissants as much as I do and has them as frequently as I do, then you will know that they can vary enormously, but hey that is all part of the fun.

The confusion over our bill did nothing to detract from the experience. We had seen signs for a theatre within the building so we took a walk upstairs to take a look, only to find another three floors of this café and a queue for the lunchtime performance at the theatre.

I have put this venue on my list of places to revisit when I am next in Dublin's fair city.

184

*

We jumped on a bus close by, after first confirming with the driver that he was going to the zoo. I was indeed feeling confident about the bus network but did not want to be over confident and end up on the wrong side of the county. I became an impromptu guide for my buddy, pointing out as much as I could remember from my various bus tours. He was not inundated with information about dates and political figures, as I retained little in those departments but at least I remembered enjoying the tours when I did them.

The end of the route found us driving through a less than savoury quarter. We were close to the entrance of Phoenix Park, where the zoo is and it was hardly surprising that the tour bus chooses not to take tourists down these streets. We drove past some dwellings with an assortment of windows. Some looked brand new, well kept, even double glazed, yet some above or on the same floor were boarded up. It was an interesting mix, with an equally interesting selection of people, some looking a little worse for wear to put it mildly. Still, looking on the bright side, at least they had a bus service.

The zoo was fun, I enjoyed it, we both enjoyed it. There were not many people there understandably, I suppose, given the unsettled weather. The first lady we tried to buy our entrance tickets from, redirected us. It looked like an entrance and it was certainly a way in but we interrupted her from behind her pane of glass, only to be told that it was the wrong counter. Down the path a bit we found another lady, behind another pane of glass, looking all set to take money but she too redirected us. Finally at the third window, money was exchanged for a map of the zoo and finally, we were allowed access. I was fairly amused by the whole process because it was early afternoon with hardly anyone around, no one else was trying to gain access but us, yet they found it necessary to have multiple forms of ticket purchase and entry. I could only assume they were rehearsing for the expected summer crowds.

Like I said, the zoo was fun, I enjoyed it, we both enjoyed it. This is the first zoo I have been to that did not smell like a zoo. Not sure how they succeeded in eliminating the characteristic aroma of animal elimination but it must be the result of a great deal of attention to a high level of cleanliness. My buddy was most excited by the hippos and I by the penguins. Well, it promised to be Happy Feet all over again, not emperors of course but a few highly inquisitive little fellas reminiscent of Ramone and his amigos. If you have seen Happy Feet then I hope you enjoyed it too, if you have not seen it then none of that will have made any sense at all.

Fascinated by a gloriously, regal, iridescent peacock just wandering about, I filmed it until it turned its back and walked down a set of steps, trailing its exquisitely long, artistic feathers behind it, like a designer ball gown and train. Why was I so surprised when it took off down the steps? I don't know, I just was. I really did not expect it to, so I was surprised when it did.

My buddy was feeling the cold and suggested we find somewhere to sit inside to warm up. According to our map there were several eating establishments, we found them all closed except one. That made our choice easier I suppose. Okay, so I did not expect it to equal the three level stained glass, embroidery velvet seated, oil painting decorated, theatre included coffee shop / restaurant but I also did not quite expect it to look like a primary school dining room either. We glanced through the window and looked at each other. He was cold and I was hungry, neither of us was thrilled by the prospect of what lay before us. At the entrance I said aloud,

"The food will be delicious, the food will be delicious, the food will be delicious."

I guess I must have sounded like I was chanting because he said,

"Is that Law of Attraction you're doing there?" I was impressed by his accuracy.

"Well," I replied, "I have no choice if I am to be joyful."

It is just as well I had focus tools at my disposal because the food on display left much to be desired. Let us just say visions of roof tiles, stones and clay, hey, that is all I am saying. I was hungry and was choosing to feel hopeful and made my selection from the one option that looked like a possibility for consumption. Looking on the bright side, my choice was actually simplified by the mere fact that, I could immediately discount all of the others. I believe in my well-being so went for it. My buddy on the other hand was taking no risks. Not even a drink, until I suggested at least a cup of tea might be worthy of consideration, to warm him from the inside. Oh how funny.

The chap who dished it up seemed happy to tell me that he was not responsible for making it and gleefully offered to give me extra. Thanks but I assured him that would not be necessary. I told the young, pretty, bored looking, blond lady at the till that it was my last day in Ireland and that I was trying not to be sad because I had enjoyed my time there. She brightened up as if remembering something. Who knows? Perhaps I had reminded her of happier days, perhaps she was thinking of days when she was less bored. I told her I would be back for another holiday and she said she was glad.

The only other customers were a lady with a small person in a high chair. We distracted ourselves from the food by enjoying the antics of the meerkats behind the glass at one end of the building. One of these delightful little creatures took his job as company lookout very seriously. He stayed upon the highest rock the entire time we were there, while the others scampered and scurried about below. They were so cute and fun to watch. I thought it was a fantastic idea to have them there as part of the dining experience and whoever thought of putting them behind the viewing wall, was a genius.

*

While meerkat watching, our man (well the Irish say 'yer man' this and 'yer man' that, so I am saying our man) asked about my sight-seeing escapades. Among other events, I told him about the friendly man I met in the grounds of Trinity College. Interestingly, my café companion had a different perspective on the whole proceedings. For example, when I told him how the chap practically ran towards me, how I had spotted him approaching at a pace, diagonally across the square through the crowds, his response was, "that's a bit weird." I agreed that he might think so but I did not, so much because it has happened to me before, so not as strange as it might seem to others.

Then I recounted the conversation and he was amused by me saying that I thought we were just chatting. He said,

"Carole, he was chatting you up." Again, I said that I thought we were just having a nice chat, which made him laugh even more. Seemingly, this meant that I was naïve and led him to ask whether I thought I might have responded differently, if I had fancied the gentleman in question. Well, how do I answer that? I really do not know how I would have responded, if someone had rung my bells, as well as talked easily and flattered charmingly. Who knows? I suspect the entire conversation may have been different and indeed his array of questions may have sat differently with me.

Anyway, I am glad that my buddy for the day was so entertained by my tale and it led me to wonder if the college grounds Romeo is a regular in that place, spotting lone females from his prime vantage point. I mean, think about it. From his chosen observation position, he sees arrivals of couples, families and singles, makes his choice, continues to observe, makes his assumptions of interests, age, appearance, intelligence, awaits signs of departure then ... pounce. Sounds like a good plan, for animals in the wild perhaps. On reflection, if he was an accomplished observer and pouncer, there would have been no need for the initial not so smooth, not so sophisticated approaching run. Perhaps it was an impulsive moment for him after all. Perhaps he was just inexplicably mesmerised by my presence and simply unable to control himself. I think I shall stay with the latter version, as it has a more fairy tale feel to it and I am a fairy tale kind of girl at heart. I can be Giselle from Disney's fabulous 'Enchanted' any day.

Still in the restaurant and talking about our dancing, my new buddy discovered that while his trip was primarily to dance at an event that just happened to be in Ireland, the fundamental reason for my trip was to be in Ireland. The dancing weekend just turned out to be a happy bonus. This was so easy for me to understand and made perfect sense to me but he seemed to puzzle over it.

"Why did you want to come to Ireland, what was attracting you so much?" That was easy to answer.

"Are you kidding me? Have you heard these people speak? Their accents are deliciously intoxicating, I had to come, to immerse myself in the sound of Irish voices." Thankfully this made a bit of sense to him. I even let him into a little known secret, that if an Irish man is speaking to me, I often am not listening to a word he is saying but am floating away on some cloud, by the voice, with my knees all of a wobble. Then he said that he feels like that when he hears a woman with an Irish accent. So there we were with something in common.

*

Back in the city, all I had left on my 'to do' list was to buy gifts from the wonderful selection in the large main tourist office in the church building. We arrived. It was closed. No worries, I had a back-up plan. My buddy wanted food and after describing what he fancied, I figured that I knew just the place. I took him to the pretty, little, rustic café where I had two days previously purchased my delicious quiche and muffin and he was delighted. Leaving him there, I back tracked to another souvenir shop, met a couple of Americans who agreed that you can never have enough key rings and the best gifts for people are biscuits and chocolate. The recipient knows you were thinking about them and they do not get lumbered with having to keep something they do not actually want, they can just eat the gift and everyone wins.

On my way back to the café, I spotted a huge green sign saying POST. It was the green of the post boxes, the uniform of the post men and the colour of the sub post offices I had seen when travelling on buses. I have no idea how I had not noticed it before, especially as I needed stamps since I bought post cards on my first day on holiday. This was obviously a main post office and luckily was still open, even though lots of other shops seemed to be closed or preparing to close.

It had two entrances and I picked one, heading straight ahead towards a gorgeous, smiling man available behind his glass screen. He looked happy

Carole Chandler

and friendly, so why was I surprised? Well, let us just say that I have been to several post offices over the years and cannot remember ever seeing anyone look quite so pleased to be working in one.

This chap was a happy chappy, content to listen to me telling him that I had bought post cards for my children several days earlier and I had not posted them yet, also how I had thought of posting them back in England but he agreed that it is not quite the same is it. I rummaged around in my purse for the selection of coins of varying denomination in order to give him the correct money. He did not mind at all that I looked at both sides of each coin to check the amount it represented because I was still, yes, still unfamiliar with the currency. I said,

"You're not in a hurry are you?" He just laughed and replied,

"No, you're fine." I had hoped he would say, 'to be sure to be sure' but it was not to be. He did however say,

"Are ya trying to get rid of yer shrapnel there, are ya?" That tickled me and made me think that he probably sees tourists do that a lot, as they prepare to leave the country. He was a cutie, an unhurried, happy, post office worker and I would have happily stayed to chat for longer but my buddy was waiting for me in the café. Well, I need not have worried because I found him just starting a vast bowl of seafood chowder. That meant that he was fine and obviously going to be a while, so I treated myself to a delicious spinach and ricotta quiche with a cup of peppermint tea to wash it down. I finished my food before he did, well I did say that he had a vast bowl.

I have no idea when he changed his mind about his lunch date which he had mentioned earlier because we had spent the whole day together. He did not mention it again and I chose not to ask. After our bus back we parted, acknowledging tremendous enjoyment in the sharing of our fabulous company, thanking each other for a lovely day, with wishes for pleasant journeys and expectations to meet again in some country or another on the tango circuit.

It is funny how things work out really. Prior to this weekend we had never met, I did not even know how to spell his name, I had not danced with him at all during the weekend, we just seemed to rendezvous and it all went well. I only say, funny because I have spent less time with people I have known longer and not had nearly so much fun.

*

I knew I had to prepare for my early morning departure but I just could not or did not want to think about it. There were not many people about considering that the weekend was officially over, people left either Sunday evening or in dribs and drabs during the Monday.

I pottered about half-heartedly packing, interspersed with reading or writing for the amusement of it. About eight o'clock I felt a sudden urge to dress and go to reception to book my cab for the morning. There was someone new at reception. Another lovely Irishman to listen to, someone else to tell just how much I had enjoyed my trip and how I did not want to leave. Well, not just yet anyway. He laughed and said that surely the weather made me want to go home and I assured him that we have rain in London too, so it was not a deciding factor. Really, I am so unbothered by the rain that I do not carry an umbrella. I stopped carrying one a few years ago about the time I started to believe in the beauty of everything, about the time I began to appreciate all weather. My constant feeling about rain is that I never get rained on and that is what I say. It works. I was wondering more and more why so many people assumed that the rain could make any difference. Why would it make any difference at all? Perhaps I was missing something.

Anyway, with the cab booked I told him that I was off to post my cards, which I had bought days before and for which I had only just bought stamps. He offered to hold them at reception for me and pop them in the post the next day. His kind suggestion he said,

"To save you the walk." I thanked him for the offer but there was no need, I was glad for the walk, wet weather or not. My son has been surprised more than once, when I have announced that I am going out for a walk,

"But it's raining," he would say as if I had not noticed.

"Yes, I know, I'm going because it's raining." Then I would disappear and not be back for ages, enjoying the fun of a refreshing walk in the rain, smelling nature and observing puddles. I seem to remember it was a walk in the rain, which inspired my new found love of painting, so there is creativity to be found in all weathers.

Anyway, I had spotted the emerald green post box during my travels and it was pretty close to the bus stop. The reception chap probably thought I was a crazy tourist for bothering but as the years go by I care less and less what people think, so I bid him adieu and left.

I had not intended to but when I accomplished my mission, I felt the urge to walk further, so I carried on down the beautiful double tree lined avenue with its gorgeous houses. After all it was my last day and after all I was still on holiday, so walking felt like a great plan. I was enjoying the smell of the wet trees, the fragrant garden flowers and the damp grass, when as I passed a big white church, I heard music playing. I stopped to listen. Did my ears deceive me or was I hearing bagpipes? I was confused. I do not like being confused. Why oh why would someone be playing bagpipes in Ireland, when I had always been led to believe that they were uniquely Scottish?

I became even more confused when I remembered seeing someone on Saturday afternoon in the city wearing a kilt and playing bagpipes outside one of the many tourist offices. When I saw him I wondered why he was there but realised that if I saw a busker in a kilt playing bag pipes in Central London I would not give it a second thought. I would have let it go, if I had not seen a group of three men soon afterwards wearing kilts. So I figured, not enough kilt wearers to make me think there was a sporting event taking place but too many kilt wearers to ignore.

So back to the avenue, my walk, the pipes and the church, I paused to listen. A woman approached and stood beside me. She paused a moment to listen too, she smiled, I smiled, I asked her if she knew what the music was for. With yet another delicious Irish accent for my entertainment, she told me that we were listening to the sound of rehearsals of the local boys' band. They practise every week and perform in the summer.

"I'm confused, are they playing bagpipes?" She told me they were (sounds like) illan pipes, they are like bagpipes but they call them illan pipes because they are played by using the elbow and illan is Irish for elbow. Oh bless her, she even went on to tell me the Irish for forearm, wrist and hand but I am sad to say that she had totally lost me by then. She was the sweetest lady and seemed happy to take the time to tell me more than I requested. I did ask her to spell what sounded like illan because I thought it would help but for some reason I became increasingly confused. I seemed to have trouble retaining the collection of letters she offered me. I was hearing illan and she gave me uelan or was it uellann or was it uilan or was it uellanne? When I returned to London I asked another Irish person to spell it for me and she offered uelanne or uilanne because the local dialect also affects the spelling. I apologise for not exactly remembering what this dear lady took the trouble to tell me. I asked her more than once and she kindly repeated it and did not seem at all bothered by my inability to process a few letters. My excuse is that I could not visualise them in connection with the sound and I am a creatively visual person.

Not missing this opportunity of course I told her that I was out enjoying a walk, on my last day of my holiday. She seemed genuinely pleased that I had enjoyed her country so much despite the weather (once again). I assured her that I was not going to allow it to dampen my spirits (pun intended). I also assured her that I intended to return. I may have said it before once or twice and here was I saying it again and still meaning it.

My walk continued to the end of the road, then down another road in a direction I had not been before making a mental note to walk here on my return visit, especially as it led me to a beautiful park of green fields and trees that looked particularly inviting.

*

Back at my room I was in a state of heightened anticipation. Why so? Well just think about it. I had already had a lovely experience and interaction with a delightful lady at the church, which would not have taken place if I had given my post cards to the gentleman at reception or if I had returned after posting the cards myself or if I had walked on the other side of the road or indeed had walked in the other direction. It is even more fun to think about it when I consider that I had packing to do and had promised myself an early night. Some may say that meeting the Irish elbow pipes lady was a coincidence. I think not.

Seriously, I was expecting something to happen, continually expecting something to happen, something magical, something wonderful, here in this beautiful place at this time on the last day of my hols. Why was I in a state of heightened expectation? Probably because that is how my life is. Things happen and each moment of every day is like a new adventure.

How far I have come. How far away it seems from those days of not having the energy to get out of bed, never mind leave the house, stricken with misery and loneliness. I have moved mountains to bring my emotional state to where I am now. I could have written several books on the whys and wherefores but I choose not to. Why? Simply because I do not want to revisit that place, that time and more importantly, it would not be conducive to my well-being to revisit those feelings.

*

So, back to my trip home, I woke up as I so often do, moments before my alarm clock rang. A teeny weeny part of me was kind of wondering if the cab would be there on time, if indeed it arrived at all because I was in Ireland, which has a reputation for sending itself up as being a tad disorganised or a bit laissez faire. Then I remembered that I could choose to believe anything I want, so told myself that they are organised and reliable and all would be well. I found myself at reception on time with my luggage and my cab was there waiting for me.

The cab driver was a lady which threw me a bit. Why? Well, because I expect my bags to be carried by the taxi driver, it is what I expect and it is what always happens, but I would never expect another lady to carry my bag. What was I to do? Was she a lady first or a driver first? Then I remembered, this was her job and she chose to do it, did she not? I let her decide. She took my suitcase and popped it in the boot of the car, perfectly capable of being the person she wanted to be, without any concerns from me.

Surprise, surprise, I told her about my stay and how much I had enjoyed it, the weather was mentioned and I learned something about equine nursing and health provisions for race horses. Her daughter sounds amazing and loves her life in this industry, after studying in England. There is so much to learn and it is rare not to glean some new nugget of information during any interaction with another. We had time to talk about my tango weekend which interested her because she knew a couple who had recently developed a love for this dance and they had told her about the event. Maybe I met them, maybe I did not, it was of no consequence. She made me laugh when I told her that I would be returning, she said,

"Try December, it will probably be sunny then." She may be right, I have fond memories of many trips to our own beautiful, lush, green Lake District also known for its water filled clouds, emptying themselves over everyone and everything during the summer months. Some of our brightest, sunniest, driest days were during holidays in November and December. She laughed at her own joke when she said it was funny to think of people coming from all over Europe for, "tango dancing in the rain in Dublin".

What was funny for me was that here was someone else who appeared to want to focus on the weather. I have lived in England all my life and am used to the way the English succeed in bringing the weather into any conversation. I thought it was considered to be a particularly English trait. Not so, not so at all, it is a characteristic of the Irish too. However, not only do these lovely, warm, friendly people talk about the weather but I met so many who apologise for it too. Bless them. Just for the record, I would like to declare that I held no person that I met on my travels as individually or collectively responsible for the elements, fair or foul.

My arrival at Dublin port was swift and cost fifty per cent more than the quoted price, which was confirmed during booking, but hey it was the last day of my holidays so I did not care. It gave me the opportunity to use the discount voucher that the guy gave me at reception, even though the fare was expected to be under the limit to redeem it. So, that was lucky then.

My lovely, friendly, cheerful driver expressed concern for my ferry journey due to the wind and rain but I did not share her concerns and assured her that all would be well. I do smile occasionally when I remember that living life in my good feeling emotional place, as I do the majority of the time, does make life so much easier and I do not worry about things like that. Wind or no wind, choppy sea or no choppy sea, I expected all to be well.

*

The young chap at the check in desk greeted me with a broad smile across his bright pink, cherubic face, on his little round head with cropped hair and not so bright eyes with a hint of redness, which suggested a fine time may have been experienced the night before. His pleasant opening line was,

"How are ya? Tis a rainy ol' day for ya isn't it?" I told him that I was leaving after a fantastic holiday, even with all this rain we were having and feigning a frown told him that I did not want to go. Handing him my ticket I held it tightly, while he pulled and I pulled it back, he laughed and happily played along. With a cheeky grin he said that he wanted to go, he could not wait to go. Turns out that he meant to leave work to go home rather than leave Ireland for another country. His flushed face looked like the symptom of a hangover but he assured me that he was just tired due to starting work at 5am or maybe he said 5.30am, either way it was an early start at silly o'clock. Mind you I have had jobs where I started at that time and do not remember being so flushed of face, so red of eyes and so glazed of expression. Feeling sorry for him, I offered to have a word with his superior on his behalf, you know to have his hours changed. I think he appreciated the gesture but convinced me that intervention would not be necessary.

Complete with his faraway dreamy look, this lovely cherub faced young man seemed confident that my case would be safe, which is just as well as I had already decided to check it in anyway. Security was a breeze with a couple of "hello, how are ya?" I wondered which bags are checked, if any. Never mind luckily I believe that all is well, so let go of any concerns which I might have had, were I to dwell on it.

I approached an escalator which was not moving and prepared to walk up it. Hey, what just happened there? As I stepped on the first step, it started to move. Was it a coincidence? Well as there is no such thing as coincidence I knew that could not be the answer. Was it my imagination? Quite likely. Was it magic? Anything is possible. Was it triggered by a sensor? Plausible. All I know is that I have never before felt an escalator begin to move, the moment I stepped on it.

*

Well, well, well, what can I say, my cruise across the water, or ferry as some prefer to call it, was uneventful and passed quickly even though I chose not to revisit the on board cinema not even to kill some time. Time is an illusion anyway and we were at Holyhead in a flash. How is that so? I do not really know. I guess it was partly because I had plenty to do, namely write my book and read The Wizard of Oz taking me from the Emerald Isle to the Emerald City.

On the boat, I chose muesli for breakfast and a cup of hot water as there was again no herbal tea available. Once more I ask the question, how is that so? The only place on the whole trip to not offer a herbal infusion as a regular choice for a hot beverage was here on this ship. Now, that was strange. I stopped carrying my own tea bags with me years ago because speciality teas are so readily available. On reflection my calling it a cruise simply was not working because if that were the case, I suspect I would have been choosing from a selection of teas both familiar and unfamiliar, from the ordinary to the exotic, or perhaps that is just wishful thinking.

I chose a table in the dining area and sat there for the entire journey. Like I said, I had plenty to do, the journey was speedy and I was not bored for a moment. I was amused by the comings and goings though. I thought intermittently about how universal law works and how everything is vibration and is responsible for how we rendezvous with others. I thought about the

Carole Chandler

reasons why we find ourselves in the same place as other people apparently at seemingly random times. I remembered something that I have read many times, *"You don't do anything. Cosmic law remember? Like attracts like."* said by Donald Shimoda, in the wonderful book, Illusions by Richard Bach. This made me give some thought to what happened while I sat where I was sitting.

I ate my breakfast at one table with a group of six lads on the table to my right. They were a lovely crowd of Irish guys, somewhat loud and a tad raucous but entertaining none the less. The safety announcements seemed to induce an increased degree of merriment as they shouted that no one was listening. They were probably right. Then just for a laugh, they started to sing *"don't rock the boat, don't tip the boat over"* followed by a group rendition of *"hooray and up she rises"* not forgetting to include, *"what shall we do with the drunken sailor"*? One particular guy was the main clown of the group and he held court as he mimicked the announcer, making me wonder who had the accent to make fun of then. With lots of laughing and their group clearly having a good time, it was hard not to laugh along with them.

There was a family of four on the table to my left, a couple sitting two tables ahead of me and another family a few tables away. Over the next half an hour all of these people left to do whatever it is that people do on cruises, I mean ferries. I had the whole area to myself for a while, the entertainment had been fun while it lasted but the solitude was equally sweet. A couple arrived with their trays of food and drink and sat at the table beside me on my right. Was I bothered? No. Was I intrigued? Yes. I glanced around to see that all the other tables were free. I counted twenty eight tables, so they could have sat anywhere but they chose to sit next to me. How wonderful that they felt drawn to me, consciously or not it was a wonderful thing and I felt honoured.

A little while later a family of three sat at the table beside me on the left. Still the other tables were free. How interesting it was to witness this behaviour, when they could have spread out and had more space we were sitting in a little huddle.

Both sets of people left me with the place to myself again reading and writing. Well blow me if the same thing did not happen once more. A family of four sat beside me on my right followed by a group of three adults who chose to sit to my left. Looking around I was amused to see that every other table was still vacant. I chuckled to myself remembering something that a wise understanding friend said once when I told her of a similar circumstance in a Birmingham restaurant,

"Ah, they just wanted to be close to you."

Perhaps they could not help themselves and whether it is true or not, it feels nice to think so and believe it, so I shall just carry on.

*

That brings me to another point of focus and something else that I keep telling myself. It is a topic of conversation which I seem to have with others about the journey. I may have said it before but I am saying it now, I just could not get excited about flying to Ireland for my holiday. It has absolutely nothing to do with discomfort of air travel, frankly that could not be further from the truth, particularly as I worked for an airline for several years and have flown all over the world on commercial as well as lesser known aircraft too.

Anyway, when planning my trip I made enquiries with the experts at high street flight centres and also attempted to arrange my flights on line and found the whole procedure unnecessarily complicated. More to the point, it was not fun and I want to have fun. So I gathered information about travelling by train and boat and hurray, I was excited again. My point now is that every time I told anyone that I travelled or planned to go by non-flying means, one of their questions would be,

"How long does it take?" I invariably responded with,

"Oh, I don't know, I don't care it's all part of the holiday and it's fun." Many people wanted exact timings, then insisted on comparing it with flying time, mostly forgetting check-in time, journeys to and from airports, baggage allowance and other related stuff.

So what is this obsession with speed guys? What is this fascination with saving time? What do people plan to do with the extra time anyway? What is scheduled for the time they save? How can the time be put to better use? I shall stop myself now, before I get lost on a rampage about the obsession with saving time, yet having none for a few minutes of meditation, or to be truly present during a conversation or receive a massage or give a massage or enjoy any of the many wonderful, life enhancing, joy giving experiences that supposedly, 'take time'.

That is enough about that. My last comment on the subject will be, when I can get excited about flying to Dublin, if I can get excited about flying to Dublin, the next time I go then I shall fly, if not, then it is the boat for me.

*

Holyhead was pretty much as I had found it on arrival the previous time, except that the wonderfully efficient lady serving at the café had been replaced by someone else. I was missing her already. Our connecting train and my reserved seating had already gone as our ferry was late, so after a short wait we were boarding the next train to Chester.

A lady arrived at my table and asked if I minded her sitting opposite me. Of course I did not mind, why would I mind? I think it would be quite an odd thing indeed for me to mind. If she had any idea at all just quite how much I enjoy meeting and talking to strangers, she would know that there was very little chance of me minding, in fact very little chance of me minding at all.

She was a large lady, quite a large lady indeed. I mention it because she had difficulty squeezing herself between the seat and the fixed table. However, squeeze she did and being wedged in, she looked like she was there for the duration. She rummaged in her bag, took things out, put things back, rearranged contents and muttered to herself. She started to remove her jacket, grunted and put it back on. As she was so wedged in, I could see her difficulty. I attempted to read my Wizard of Oz (another thoroughly good read I might add) but it was hard not to notice this quite unsettled woman, who was all of a fidget, like a bored child.

The snack trolley arrived. She selected a Fanta and a packet of cheese and onion crisps. Interesting. Then it began. The vendor asked her for two pounds something, she gave him money plus extra she said, "to make it easier." The change was not what she expected, an argument ensued. With a series of "I gave you...", "no, you gave me...", "I assure you I gave you...", "I promise you I gave you...", "you didn't give me..." and variations thereof, the whole carriage was treated to an increasingly uncomfortable and escalating verbal exchange.

I was at the same table, I was not a good witness as I did not see the coins which were passed from one to the other. All I know is that the interaction was far from pleasant. She was sure, he was sure, she asked him to check, he assured her he was right, she knew she was positive, he doubted, she promised, and on and on and on.

It appeared that ultimately the dispute was over a pound. Not that it was any of my business, my personal conclusion was, oh for goodness sake, we clearly have an unhappy customer here, just give the poor woman her pound and explain the situation (misunderstanding or otherwise) to your boss. Give her the pound already and put everyone out of their misery. I wondered if it were really worth the time and effort already spent with this undoubtedly unhappy lady.

He trundled off with his squeaky trolley and she tried to open up the event for discussion with me. I was not inspired to get involved, so I smiled and continued to read my book. She fought with the bottle of Fanta, she battled with the packet of crisps. Such aggression taken out on inanimate objects and here was I on the same table, half expecting to be sprayed or showered at any moment. I witnessed an agitated method of imbibing and food consumption. The bottle cap was frantically twisted and turned several times, a swig taken, followed by a furious succession of twists and turns to replace the lid. Next was a delving session into the crisp packet, like something from a fantasy adventure story, where the protagonist is required to dig, dig, dig, deeper and deeper and deeper into a seemingly bottomless every day object, to discover the magical prize. Hey, what do I know about it? Perhaps that is what the crisp eating, fizzy drink swigging experience is like for her.

Several minutes later, the squeaky trolley returned with the man from the earlier not so entertaining, incorrect change episode. He stopped beside my cap twisting, packet rustler and said,

"I've checked and I know that I gave you the right change but I have decided to give you the pound anyway." Yay! I was delighted and relieved, now the whole unhappy incident would be resolved, she would be pleased and I could remain in my seat without fear of flying food. To my utter amazement she said,

"No, it's alright." Then there was another bouncing back and forth of "take it", "don't want it", "I'm giving it to you", "don't be silly", "it's yours", "it's not necessary". What on earth was going on? I hardly knew. It was like a poorly written comedy sketch. Mind you if it had involved Miranda Hart it would have been brilliant. It transpired that he continued to offer to make amends his way, she continued to refuse to be accept his offer of reconciliation, so a stalemate was inevitable.

After he trundled off the second time, she made another half-hearted attempt to include me in discussions and once more I did not feel inspired to get involved. Well to be fair, if I was not interested in sharing her conflict the first time, I was unlikely to show an interest after her second round in the ring. I looked at her, smiled and continued to read my book.

Following further tussles with her snack, she asked me what I was reading, we had a brief exchange about the joy of finding a good book, she complimented me on my bracelets, I thanked her, she paid similar attention to my necklace, I thanked her and she fidgeted until we arrived at Bangor. She announced it was her stop, de-wedged herself from her seat, paused, looked at me and said,

"Thank you very much for letting me sit with you."

Well if I were so inclined, I could probably spend much time analysing the whole sequence of events but I shall leave that to others. It did however, help me to realise what my lovely, cute, young gentleman friend on the ferry over had meant, when he said that he found me to be peaceful and chilled out on the train and boat. My initial reaction was to think that it would be hard to appear to be anything else, sitting on a train or wandering around on a boat with not much to do. My table sharer on this train had demonstrated otherwise. The Universe lines us up with others, sometimes we have something to learn from them, sometimes we have something to teach. I certainly learned things from her.

I wonder whether it was something about the energy of that particular seat because she left and a young chap arrived with a large holdall and sat opposite me beside the window. Then the whole rummaging, taking things out, putting things in, rearranging scenario started all over again. He set out an array of magazines upon the table, along with his iPhone and Blackberry (well that is what they looked like and I do not claim to be an expert), he looked at me, smiled, nodded, then settled back with his head on his scarf and closed his eyes for a nap.

*

Changing at Chester was an amusing event as no one knew where to catch the next train. We waited beside a train which said Euston but we were confused because the doors would not open. I asked a passing guard who seemed to have no information either, so I told another lady who laughed and we agreed to be lost and confused together. There was a crowd of passengers on the platform and another lady asked me which train was for Euston. I told her about the inconclusive response from the station employee, showed her the sign on the train and told her that the doors were remaining firmly closed. She expressed a few opinions about the state of the nation's railway system and as I felt unable to agree, I smiled and listened without responding. She left me and soon found someone else to complain with. Meanwhile, another guard reported back to a few of us, no general loudspeaker announcement for the waiting populace, just a discreet word to the chosen few it would appear. A couple of us walked to the far end of the train where there were fewer people, in the hope of bagging a good seat with more room, when we were finally allowed to board.

Happy with my seat, I settled for the journey. Two young ladies and an older man arrived already discussing whether we were in first class or not. Well in my imagination I am always in first class but that is another story for another day. Seriously though, back to the physical reality, Virgin trains may be good but they are not that good. How could anyone have thought that we had accidentally drifted into the first class carriage? I guess it depends what you are used to.

The man sat a couple of rows away and the girls sat directly across the aisle from me. Well, these two young ladies must have been the Chester to Euston entertainers. It was impossible not to overhear their conversations which sadly were mostly devoted to their joint disapproval of the relationship choices of their friends. With a continuing cycle of what he said to her and what she did to him, it was the stuff of soap operas and I found it surprising the number of people they knew, who according to them were in failing relationships. Their conversation would not have been my ideal listening choice but I was unable to change the channel, so resorted to my superior skills of focus, to put my mind in a different place.

When they finished exposing and restoring the perceived wrong doings of others, they put their laptop on the table and without headphones proceeded to listen to a well-known stand-up comedian. It was loud enough not merely for their own personal gratification but for the whole carriage to enjoy or endure, depending on your perception.

I feel inspired to share my focus skill briefly, as it is particularly effective and easy to implement. I honed it during my frequent bus travels in our vibrant south west London, when encountering youngsters with music audible through their headphones, or better still playing via speakers on their phone or other listening device. Music played on public transport may not suit all passengers, I say 'may not' in an attempt to be tactful. When subjected to the persistent tsh chk chk tssssh, tsh chk chk tssssh, tsh chk chk, tsh chk chk, tsh chk chk tssssh, of some unknown tune, I developed a method of being content with it, instead of being annoyed by it. Realising that they have a steady rhythm I use the beat to breathe along to the repetition and enjoy an open eyed meditation, counting my inspiration and expiration courtesy of the on board metronome. It works, it is brilliant, it benefits me and I have fun.

Now admittedly it is a slightly different matter when the song lyrics are audible, particularly when the vocabulary is less then savoury. No judgement intended, just not to my taste perhaps. What do I do then? How do I cope then? I hum along and change the words. It works, it is brilliant, it benefits me and I have fun. I simply change the words to something I am happy to think about and sing about. I surprise myself with quite how easy it is to do. There is no need to be concerned about rhyming quality or sentence structure. I am not planning to submit it for examination, it is purely for my immediate amusement and long term sanity. Anyway, these are the skills which I called upon to help me focus while these young ladies seemed oblivious to the presence of anyone else in the carriage.

The particular comedian they selected for their enjoyment is well known for his angry view of politics, racial matters, women and people generally. He is not known for his warmth or political correctness. His mode of expression, choice of vocabulary and their volume were hard to ignore and the gentleman sitting opposite me expressed his objection with tuts and glares but we were all too British to complain directly.

It is good to laugh about it now, but really! I am known for my patience, I am complimented regularly for my patience. Let us look at the facts here. I am not a hermit, I have lived and continue to live with other people. Before I knew better, I tried asking for changes, however, my requests for modified behaviour have been seldom granted. Let us just say that I have learned that I do not need others to alter their actions in order for me to feel better. My ability to focus, stay positive and love everyone has not been without distraction, ergo the two lasses on the train were a picnic for me. Their conduct may have been unnecessary and unwanted but as is always the case, it came to an end. All was well.

*

I was back in London. Yay! Of course I had enjoyed my holiday but I had to leave Ireland, so that I can have the pleasure of going back. It is always good to be in my home town. I had missed the fruit bowls outside the shops. I had missed the feel of the crowds. I had loved my time in Dublin and I love London but they feel quite different. I had missed the abundance of people of colour, ooh so many colours. I had not even realised that on my trip, I saw about three people a day with dark skin and they were all in the city and looked professionally dressed in suits and smart shoes. At no time was it an issue. At no time did anyone seem bothered or surprised by my skin colour being darker than theirs. Never mind that, I had also missed our wonderful red buses, it was good to be back on one, I know how they work.

I was still in holiday mode so undecided about whether to go straight home or not. At Euston, a number 59 pulled up so I made the impromptu decision to go to my favourite restaurant in Streatham. The driver was a darling and gave me a lovely big smile with a friendly hallo as I walked past him to take my place downstairs at the back of the bus. A woman sat opposite me wearing a fuchsia pink scarf, matching trousers and coordinating bright pink finger nails. She scanned me up and down. When I smiled at her she looked away. When she thought I was not looking, she resumed her scan, from my hair down to my shoes then back up again. I smiled at her again and she looked away again. I did not mind her behaviour, I was having fun. We continued our gaze aversion dance until she got off at Brixton.

How funny, I thought. I did not remember anyone doing that in Dublin. I was missing my beloved Ireland already. I was missing the accents already. I was missing the people already. Off the bus at Streatham I passed people in the street and no matter what they looked like, for each of them I pondered, 'are you Irish', 'are you Irish', 'she looks Irish', 'so does he'.

I really was not ready to go home yet, still too excited to officially end the holiday by walking through my front door. I figured that as long as I stayed out then I was still on vacation. That's right isn't it? I went to the café with the intention of telling everyone that I had just returned from my hols and had an amazing time. Instead, I sat quietly enjoying a delicious pot of Jasmine tea, an equally delicious plate of yummy food and wrote lists upon lists of things, which I appreciated about my recent adventures. I had a lot to be thankful for and writing it all down was easy and felt so good.

My last bus home gave me a welcome opportunity to rendezvous with a driver who exchanged pleasantries, more than just a hallo, more than a nod. He appeared to have the time and the inclination to hear a little about my trip and to tell me how he has never been to the Emerald Isles but would love to go.

I stepped through my front door and my holiday officially came to an end. No sadness only joy. I have wonderful memories and am already looking forward to returning. My son, bless him, was pleased to see me, he even listened while I rattled on and on about my glorious adventures. He coped well during my absence, so I was absolutely right to trust in his common sense and believe that he would be fine. Just for the record, the kitchen was spotless and his bathroom was spotless. I make no comment and leave you to draw your own conclusions.

I did not bother to unpack, there was plenty of time for that. I had plenty to look forward to, now that I was back home. Writing my book would be like one long testimonial, there were clients to see, massages to give and meditation inspired art to create. My life is great.

*

The next three days were awesome. The next three days saw me meeting people who were somehow connected with Ireland. Some might say coincidence, I think not.

At a restaurant I chatted to a chef who is from Galway. She had just been conversing with a colleague who is planning a trip to Ireland. A couple came in who were Irish. I had a client who had just returned from Cork. I overheard a conversation on a bus about a lady's relative in Ireland. A particular heart throb of mine at Salsa turns out to be half Irish. Ah so that goes some way to explaining why he is so absolutely gorgeous, especially those dreamy eyes. Once again I kept that opinion to myself. I started to tell him about the fantastic time I had and he said,

"You always have a fantastic time." I wondered what made him say that and he continued, "You told me before that you always have a great time wherever you go." Why was I surprised that he remembered that, when I did not remember saying it?

So there you have it. I talk to strangers to be sure, to be sure, to be sure. I was in a good feeling emotional place before I went, I stayed in my good feeling emotional place while I was there and I have been in a good feeling emotional place since my return. Well pretty much, I am only human after all and sometimes things happen which may not be quite to my taste. I have learned not to worry about those moments which tend to be brief periods because now I have learned the joy of getting back to my happy place.

By way of explanation, I appreciate that there may be some inconsistency of tense in my sentences, sometimes past sometimes present. I make no excuses and offer no apology, it is just a reflection of how I felt in the moment. I allow my feelings to be my guide. Also, throughout my book I acknowledge that there are certain words which I tend to use. More than once I may have found something or someone amazing, beautiful, delightful, fantastic, gorgeous, lovely or even wonderful. Again, I make no excuses and offer no apology. It is simply a reflection of me and how I see the world, how I view my world, life from my perspective.

A few years ago I cut a quote from a magazine and put it up in the kitchen to remind myself often of its message, *'there is beauty in everything but not everybody sees it'*. I try to see it. Recently a friend asked if I live in an alternate universe and without a shadow of a doubt I assured him that I do.

Until a few years ago my world was quite different, even the opposite. There was little to enjoy, no beauty to see, nothing wonderful to experience. I was tired, unwell and miserable and hardly aware of it. Now I know that emotional wellbeing equals physical wellbeing.

Finding *Law of Attraction* has changed my life. I will rephrase that, it has not changed me, it has taught me how to be me, to be authentic, the real me. Now that I am *'finally allowing myself to be me'*, I have learned how to let go of limiting beliefs and allow all manner of good things just flow my way. My life was transformed when I stumbled across the *Teachings of Abraham* lovingly brought to us by Esther and Jerry Hicks. They say that words do not teach and we teach by the power of our example, so I offer here examples of my experiences. The way people respond to me has totally changed, I am still surprised by it occasionally and it brings me great joy. Anyone can change the way people respond to them. Anyone can turn around their view of the world. Anyone can alter the way their fortunes unfold. All of this is available to everyone, if they want it.

I learned to be open to the possibility that there may be another way of thinking. Then I made the profound decisions to -

1.   not care what anyone else thinks.

2.   remember the power of feeling good, now.

3.   meditate daily

After a whole life time of caring what people think, unconsciously seeking, needing, looking for approval, it takes focus to stop making the opinion of others a priority.

After regularly feeling negative emotion, it sounds simple but takes some effort to just believe that it is okay to even want to feel good.

I developed an alternative view of life, a new view of the world. I had a glimpse of the life I wanted. From my place of feeling profoundly unseen, unheard, unworthy and unloved, I knew that something had to change and I had to make it happen. I could not rely on anyone else.

Introduction to *Law of Attraction* begins for most people with the search for improvements in health, wealth, relationships and career and not necessarily in that order. My initial quest was no different. Now it is all about continually striving to just feel better. Sounds simple? It takes focus. I focus my thoughts, I focus my attention. That is where the work is. That is where the effort is. The rest I leave to the Universe.

It works every time for me, for everyone, without exception. It is a belief that remains consistent and is the only thing that I have ever discovered for personal guidance that makes sense. I have learned how to follow our own inner guidance. We all have our own guidance and when (if and when) we choose to follow it, it will guide us correctly every time.

I feel I have come to a natural close with my book today, so perhaps in my next book I may say something more about how people used to respond to me, family, friends, colleagues and strangers. I may feel an inclination to say more about how I turned my expectations around.

For now, I feel inspired to say:

We all get to choose. My life is what I make it. You choose yours. Enjoy.

* * * * * * *

Thank you to my wonderful children, who continue to teach and inspire me every moment of every day. Bless you both.

Thank you to the Wholemeal Café angels, for creating a divine space and keeping me fed and watered during my many hours of writing. Bless you all.

Thank you to everyone I have ever met no matter how brief the interaction. Without all of you I would not be the person I am today and these books would not exist.

Just for fun, you will find information about my energy balancing treatments on www.massageforinnerpeace.co.uk where I have also have listed some of the books and music which have contributed to my journey. However top of my reading list is *'Ask And It Is Given – The Teachings of Abraham'*, Esther and Jerry Hicks as well as *'Illusions – The Adventures of a Reluctant Messiah'*, Richard Bach. Top of my listening list is anything by *Sacred Earth Music*, Prem and Joshua Williams.

If you fancy a little further browsing, you will find examples of my meditation inspired art on www.celestialcircles.co.uk

A wise person once said, *'If it feels good it is good, if it doesn't it isn't'*

I wish you everything I wish for myself, joy, love and peace.

Carole

In Dublin's fair city

Where the people are witty

I focus my hearing on accents alone

With goodbye and hello

And characters mellow

I love it there and I am going back soon

I'm going back soon

I'm going back soon

I love it there and I am going back soon